The DIY
Filmmaker

Life Lessons for Surviving Outside Hollywood

Paul Peditto & Boris Wexler

Self-Counsel Press
(a division of)
International Self-Counsel Press Ltd.
USA   Canada

Self-Counsel Press acknowledges the financial support of the Government of Canada through the Canada Book Fund for our publishing activities.

Printed in Canada.

First edition: 2015

Library and Archives Canada Cataloguing in Publication

Peditto, Paul, author
    The DIY filmmaker / Paul Peditto and Boris Wexler.

(Reference series)
Issued in print and electronic formats.
ISBN 978-1-77040-221-8 (pbk.).—ISBN 978-1-77040-990-3 (epub).—ISBN 978-1-77040-991-0 (kindle)

    1. Motion pictures—Production and direction. 2. Motion pictures—Distribution. 3. Motion picture authorship. 4. Amateur films—Production and direction. I. Wexler, Boris, author II. Title. III. Title: Do-it-yourself filmmaker. IV. Series: Self-counsel reference series

| PN1995.9.P7P43 2015 | 791.4302'32 | C2014-908255-X |
| | | C2014-908256-8 |

Foreword provided by Josef Steiff, used with permission.
Light and Sufferer case study in the download kit by Christopher Peditto, used with permission.
Chapter 9, Marketing and Distribution, information provided by the guest author, Carolina Posse, used with permission.

Self-Counsel Press
(a division of)
International Self-Counsel Press Ltd.

| Bellingham, WA | North Vancouver, BC |
| USA | Canada |

Contents

Download kit

Table

Notice to Readers

Laws are constantly changing. Every effort is made to keep this publication as current as possible. However, the author, the publisher, and the vendor of this book make no representations or warranties regarding the outcome or the use to which the information in this book is put and are not assuming any liability for any claims, losses, or damages arising out of the use of this book. The reader should not rely on the author or the publisher of this book for any professional advice. Please be sure that you have the most recent edition.

Note: The fees quoted in this book are correct at the date of publication. However, fees are subject to change without notice.

Prices, commissions, fees, and other costs mentioned in the text or shown in samples in this book probably do not reflect real costs where you live. Inflation and other factors, including geography, can cause the costs you might encounter to be much higher or even much lower than those we show. The dollar amounts shown are simply intended as representative examples.

Website links often expire or web pages move, at the time of this book's publication the links were current.

For Brenda Webb at Chicago Filmmakers, and Joe Steiff at Columbia College, who turned an Aurora riverboat craps-dealer into a screen-writing teacher, and who started this whole damn thing.

— Paul Peditto

For Julian Grant who taught me most of the principles I discuss in this book, and for the cast and crew of Fall Away, Roundabout American, *and* Chat, *who made the filming of these projects an unforgettable experience.*

— Boris Wexler

Foreword:
Surviving outside Hollywood

When I got my first office and phone number, there was little more exciting than recording my outgoing voicemail greeting. I was a burgeoning filmmaker, eager to start, ready for the calls to start pouring in. And I did get a lot of calls; they just weren't for me.

My new phone number had belonged to someone else before me — another filmmaker, no less. What are the odds? With each voicemail from increasingly irate creditors, I slowly began to piece together what had happened. He was one of those filmmakers who had been inspired by Spike Lee to make a feature on credit cards — sure he'd be able to sell the finished film, sure he'd pay off his cards and make a little money. Unfortunately, when he finished the film, it did not get distribution, barely showed in any festivals, and caused him to sink into a mass of debt that followed him — and filled my voicemail — for years.

That was when I first realized how risky filmmaking really is, how important it is to ground my passion, how necessary it is to take a hard look at the resources at hand and make them work for me rather than against me. That's why I'm so excited for this book, the one in your hands. Paul, Boris, and Carolina do this every day with their own projects and are here to help you do the same with yours.

For many of us, we start out aspiring to make films like Hollywood or similar entities. This makes total sense because these are the films we are most exposed to. But we don't always realize that Hollywood's notions of filmmaking are often unreasonable for us to emulate. Studios spread their risk over multiple films (the successes counterbalancing the failures) while film boards minimize their risk with subsidies. For us outside Hollywood, we don't have these benefits — we're usually fully invested in one film at a time, each venture potentially "make or break."

Hollywood producers regularly tell me there's only one way to make films, and that it's impossible to make a movie for less than $20 million. Neither is true for those of us outside Hollywood, but many believe this, and it can lead us to overreach or give up.

However, there's a middle ground that has come into view as access to high-quality equipment has become more affordable, computers are able to do the work that once required specialized machines, and software has become more sophisticated. Navigating this middle ground is the challenge before us, and it is an exciting time to be making films. We can create new models, learn from our peers, experiment, and take reasonable risks. This book can help us take those first steps, to find our direction and to roll camera.

Paul and Boris redefine micro-budget to reflect our individual circumstances and resources, to take stock of what is within our reach, and to maximize "doing it our own way." Whether you're about to embark on your first film or your tenth, you will find many helpful tips, perspectives, and firsthand experience to help you realize your vision. Making a film is always a gamble, but this book helps stack the odds in your favor.

Surviving outside Hollywood is possible and this book will show you how.

— Josef Steiff

Josef Steiff is a writer and independent filmmaker whose films have been exhibited in the United States, Europe, and Asia. He wrote and directed the award-winning feature *The Other One* as well as the short films *Borders, Catching Fire, Eclipse, I Like My Boyfriend Drunk,* and *How*

Will I Tell? Surviving Sexual Assault. As a producer, he line produced the feature length More Beautiful than a Flower for MBC (Korea) and coproduced Rhapsody. He currently oversees the MFA Programs in Creative Producing and Cinema Directing at Columbia College Chicago.

Introduction

Do you need to be in Los Angeles to consider yourself a filmmaker? No.

Do you need to be in Los Angeles to start your career as a screenwriter? No.

Do you need to have an agent or a manager to place well in screenwriting contests, to be coached by screenwriting gurus, and attend screenwriting conferences to start your career as a filmmaker?

No, no, and NO!

I stand before you a true convert to the new religion: Do-It-Yourself Filmmaking. This is not a new church. Low-budget movies have been around since William K.L. Dickson filmed Fred Ott's Sneeze in 1894.[1] John Cassavetes made films for low money. So did Orson Welles, who made bad wine commercials to finance his low-budget Shakespeare adaptations. Robert Rodriguez literally wrote the book about low-budget films, and major directors such as Spike Lee and Darren Aronofsky got their starts on the cheap. Credit card filmmaking has been around forever, the watchword being *film* making. These early low-budget efforts

---

1 *Sneeze*, filmed by William K.L. Dickson, starring Fred Ott, accessed February 2015.
  https://www.youtube.com/watch?v=5fbXzM6hka4

were all shot on film — which brings us to what is new in the equation: Digital Technology.

What is new is being able to pick up a Canon 7D, or an ALEXA, or a Red Digital Cinema Camera, and shoot a movie saying *exactly* what you want to say, and maintaining *control* of both content and distribution. Also new are digital platforms to sell your product that didn't exist ten years ago. These platforms have leveled the playing field and democ-ratized the entire process of the art. We take these rapid advances for granted. It's the speed of the change that is often truly breathtaking, and the wonder of where it all will lead.

So what's any of this got to do with you, Good Reader? Hollywood. Home of the true 1 percent. Behind this gated community are the kidney-shaped pools, impeccable hedgerows, million-dollar mansions, and Lamborghini excess — the Country Club of which you are most definitely not a member. You cannot apply to this club. The gatekeepers know you are not of their cloth. They can smell you. You are the Un-washed. They can feel your wanting, your desperation to join them on the inside. They have set up impenetrable motes and ramparts to stop you. How will you scale these walls?

For your part, you have played by the rules. You wrote query letters to find an agent, followed the message boards, paid through the nose to take advice from the gurus, and bought their books even though it didn't much seem to help. You sent into as many screenwriting contests as you could, put your scripts on websites that claimed the inside ear of "industry professionals" — meaning the 1 percent. You did all these things with a belief in your work as a writer. You just wanted a chance, a chance to … what? To have an agent, take meetings, pitch and get sent on assignment work, work your way into the Writers Guild, pump out one, two, or five movies, establish a reputation, and get on the board! You dream of making it inside that Hollywood gate. You've tried every "old school" method, but old school is dead.

Don't go to Los Angeles until you're invited. I know this runs counter to what you read on the Internet. I throw this out there as a way to get you to start thinking about yourself and what alternatives you have at your disposal.

Is Los Angeles a place where you could live? How are you planning on surviving for years? Yes, *years*! It will take time before your career takes off doing it the traditional way. What about trying to write in your home city? Here in Chicago, Illinois, we've currently got six network TV shows shooting on our sound stages. There is infrastructure in terms of locations — major and independent (indie) movies shoot here all the time because there are great tax incentives provided by this movie-friendly state. There are seasoned crews and great acting schools spawning excellent actors. However, there actually isn't plenty of production money here. Sure, lots of TV and indies get made here, but where does the money to pay for these shows come from? It's impossible to deny that the majority of production companies, agencies, and managers are based in LA. The industry is in LA and has been for almost 100 years ago. With the mechanism of Hollywood so entrenched, how the heck do you make it anywhere other than LA?

Understand what it is you write. If you're thinking of going to LA, the stuff you're writing should be in tune with what they buy. Being a former casino craps dealer, I believe in playing the odds. So, if I tell you that less than 200 spec scripts were bought last year while approximately 100,000 were registered, you can see that the odds are stacked against you. Especially if we consider that your script is an autobiographical, character-driven, passion piece about your Uncle Joe's bankrupt Cleveland bowling alley circa 1954. I know, you wrote it with passion, with verve, with memories and insight, and magic! Cool. Now pitch the concept in a sentence. Because if you can't, it's likely you'll be bucking the odds in a town that wants pitches that are four words or less such as *Abraham Lincoln, Vampire Hunter*, or *Snakes on a Plane*.

Sure, it's possible your fabulous spec will find its way to the right producer. Happens every year. But if you're headed to LA, do yourself a favour and consider the odds. The number of specs made via Studio or Indie productions each year is in the very low hundreds. Versus the 100,000-plus registered. This isn't me telling you to give up your dream. It's me telling you to know what you're facing when you go to Hollywood. who will unlock the right doors. It's also possible it won't.

Look at your material. Are you writing the big concept stuff a studio will want? If not, do you have the connections to find a sympathetic producer to go the indie route? While there's no specific numbers defining an indie budget, it's safe to say 2 million to 20 million would be a common range. That number will determine the "bankable name talent" you can attract. It's an ever-changing algorithm: How much is your "star" actually worth?

Which brings us to the eternal Catch-22: You need a star to get financing for your million-dollar movie, but no star will be interested in the project without that money already in the bank. If you manage to ask about their "name" client, the first question to you will be: "Is it funded?" But how do you get the money without the name? I've known multiple hopeful filmmakers who have tried to beat this implacable logic, who chased name talent for ten or more years.

Fortunately, Good Reader, there is another way to make your Uncle Joe's bowling alley movie. Micro-budget. There's no simple definition of what micro-budget is. It goes something like: Micro-budget is whatever you can pull from your pocket, or the pockets of your family or the pockets of every friend you ever had when you beg for cash during your 30-day Kickstarter campaign. Micro-budget is the money you directly control, without strings. The unlimited "write-your-dream-first-draft" budget has no place here. What you raise is what you had better write as a movie.

Meanwhile you need to be doing something else: Develop a network of people who can help make the script happen. That means networking within your filmmaking community. Go to events and other people's films, meeting directors of photography (DPs), production designers, editors, and other filmmakers who are starting their careers. Sure, it helps Seek out organizations in your city that connect filmmakers; in Chicago, for instance, we have Chicago Filmmakers. Take a class, network, and get educated.

Learn, too, about the mechanisms in place to help you raise money. Kickstarter and Indiegogo help thousands of grassroots do-it-yourself efforts get off the ground. They are responsible for the $25,000 campaign that my cowriter, Boris Wexler, and I ran for our movie, *Chat*. See the download kit for The Making of *Chat*, which includes pictures and notes about our process.

Fundraise through Kickstarter, through family and friends, or any resource at your disposal. If the script is written with micro-budget cost savings in mind, making the movie is absolutely within your reach.

You can make your movie in Idaho, Iowa, or Ohio! Write a script that makes it into Sundance Film Festival and you won't ever need to write a query letter again. You will field calls from agents and managers. And you, too, will be allowed entrance into the Hollywood Country Club. That's what this book is about: Doing it on your terms.

Chapter one

Life Lessons for Surviving outside Hollywood

What kind of movies do you write? Are they mass-market, monster concept scripts? Are they art-house style, Sundance-type character-driven pieces? Are they niche market, micro-budget stories that can be made for a budget that you raise yourself? Do you need to live in LA? Failure to ask these questions will lead to years going by without success, with even the most optimistic writer being chipped away, and the most hopeful losing hope.

Identify what you're writing, and find a workable strategy for you to get your work out there.

It's an oversimplification to say there are three categories of movies you can write, but just to get our arms around this, I'd like to organize the focus on three different markets of movies which are studio, indie, and micro-budget.

1. Three Paths to Glory

William Faulkner and F. Scott Fitzgerald wrote novels that will be around 500 years from now. Yet when it came time to write screenplays, they struggled within the Hollywood studio system. Producing literary works that stood the test of time was a cakewalk compared to pumping out dreck for the studio bosses who wrote them huge checks. A devil's bargain indeed.

Screenwriter and playwright David Mamet said it best some years ago, "Film is a collaborative business: bend over."[1]

The Hollywood studio system of the 1940s and 1950s is part of cinema history. If we go back 20 years to the early 1990s, the indie wave of Quentin Tarantino, Spike Lee, and Kevin Smith, are also part of cinematic history. In 2015 another path is fully established: Micro-Budget. Filmmakers need to be which path to walk. This depends on what they have to say and how much money they need to say it.

Let's look at the three paths as of 2015:

- **Studio movies:** Remakes, reboots, sequels, comic book and graphic novel adaptations, board games and toy movies, branded entertainment. These can range from $20 million to $200 million, including their marketing budgets. Cross-platform marketing possibilities such as fast food restaurants giving away toys and prizes tied into the movies being promoted.

- **Indie movies:** Generally, a low-end indie could be considered $500,000 and a high-end indie up to $20 million. These movies have more leeway creatively. They almost always require bankable names to finance. The search for a star can last years, getting the money in the bank is the quest. People will swear their interest is real but as a producer friend once defined it, the money is real "when I'm eating the steak from the check that has cleared."

- **Micro-budget movies:** This is a world filled with no-name actors, budget limitations, and drama upon drama that comes from never having enough money when you make the movie. But a few of them will make a noise, and the filmmakers wouldn't have had that opportunity without the technological or marketplace innovations of just the last few years. This book is about how to give yourself the best chance in that environment. If you bought this book you're interested in exploring this path. But

---

1 *The Devil's Guide to Hollywood: The Screenwriter as God!* (2006), Joe Eszterhas.

before you do you must be clear on the movie you're writing, the audience and the marketplace. Once the "fun" of writing the thing is over, the selling of the toothpaste begins.

Let's take a look at each of these in more detail.

1.1 Studio movies

Studio-budgeted movies are the tent poles, the sequel/prequel, reboot/remake, A-list populated, branded product, mega-$$$ projects that, by definition, leave spec scriptwriters entirely out of the equation. These are the "big six" studios:

- Paramount Pictures
- Walt Disney Studios
- 20th Century Fox
- Warner Bros.
- Columbia Pictures
- Universal Studios

With the recent trend toward $200 million movies there are fewer of these being made. The unknown screenwriter doesn't get these assignments; and the vast majority of Writers Guild of America (WGA) members don't get this work, either. The number of consistently working writers seems to diminish with each passing year.

It's not the purpose of this book to discourage you from taking any path, including this one. If you're writing mega-budget thrillers such as *Terminator* or *Tomb Raider*, you'll want to go the LA route, which means finding an agent, taking meetings, pitching for assignment work, etc. If your stuff is studio budget, then you'll need the studios to make it happen. That means being part of the system.

My screenplays have never been considered at the studio level — even when I was with William Morris and Writers & Artists, it didn't happen. Frankly, the movie studios want and bankroll the properties I was not writing. This isn't false modesty, just honesty, and it's essential. You have got to be honest with yourself. What kind of movies are you writing? The answer to that question will determine your course of action.

If you want to write for the big-six studios, your script will need a killer concept, probably adapted from preexisting material with a built-in

Table 1
TOP 20 GROSSING MOVIES IN 2012*

Movie	Studio	Total Gross in Domestic Theaters	Opening Week-end in Domestic Theaters
Marvel: The Avengers	Buena Vista	$623,357,910	$207,438,708
The Dark Knight Rises	Warner Bros.	$448,139,099	$160,887,295
The Hunger Games	Lionsgate	$408,010,692	$152,535,747
Skyfall	Sony Pictures	$304,360,277	$88,364,714
The Hobbit: An Unexpected Journey	Warner Bros.	$303,003,568	$84,617,303
The Twilight Saga: Breaking Dawn Part 2	Lionsgate	$292,324,737	$141,067,634
The Amazing Spider-Man	Sony Pictures	$262,030,663	$62,004,688
Brave	Buena Vista	$237,283,207	$66,323,594
Ted	Universal Pictures	$218,815,487	$54,415,205
Madagascar 3: Europe's Most Wanted	Paramount Pictures	$216,391,482	$60,316,738
Dr. Suess' The Lorax	Universal Pictures	$214,030,500	$70,217,070
Wreck-It Ralph	Buena Vista	$189,422,889	$49,038,712
Lincoln	Buena Vista	$182,207,973	$944,308
MIB 3	Sony Pictures	$179,020,854	$54,592,779
Django Unchained	Weinstein Company	$162,805,434	$30,122,888
Ice Age: Continental Drift	20th Century Fox	$161,321,843	$46,629,259
Snow White and the Huntsman	Universal Pictures	$155,332,381	$56,217,700
Les Misérables	Universal Pictures	$148,809,770	$27,281,735
Hotel Transylvania	Sony Pictures	$148,313,048	$42,522,194
Taken 2	20th Century Fox	$139,854,287	$49,514,769

*Source: Dollar amounts from Box Office Mojo, http://boxofficemojo.com/yearly/chart/?yr=2012

audience and demographic. Table 1 is a list of the top 20 grossing movies for 2012 and the studios that produced them.

1.2 Indie movies

If you're not writing for the studios, who will you target? It might be the "mini-majors" (e.g., Weinstein Company, Lionsgate, MGM) who produce their share of genre-based films, but also the character-driven movies that get a buzz during Oscar time.

The budget for indie films is almost always less than for studio movies. Although there is no standard definition, a movie costing from $1 million to $20 million is in the ballpark for indies. If you want to know what these movies look like, go to Moviefone's website (http://news.moviefone.com/2012/02/25/independent-spirit-awards/).

What will the movie you're writing cost? If it's within the indie level, it means you, or a producer interested in your project, will need — not want, *need* — A-level talent to bankroll the movie and market it on completion.

Are there rare cases of angel financing for vanity projects in the million-dollar range? Sure. I don't want to seem strident here, but for the majority of indie-movie producers will need a name actor (or more than one name actor) signed and sealed for your script to see the light of day. Not just any name either but a bankable name — someone who will put people in the theater seats at $12 per ticket. That means the protagonist and antagonist that you write about have to be marketable. It also puts you square into the classic Catch-22 of movie financing: You need a name to finance the movie but you can't get the name until the film is financed. There are no absolutes. Maybe you'll call an agent and pitch your new thriller to the assistant's assistant. Maybe he or she will listen to your phone pitch without interruption and ask you to send the script. Maybe the person will love it, sign you as a client, and package the movie with A-list talent, the movie will be well-received, even Oscar-consideration and … maybe the proverbial "pigs will fly"!

Without the ability to make a pay-or-play offer, the agent isn't going to prioritize your script for a client to read. Why would the agent? An agent is sitting on a pile of funded scripts to consider. The purpose of this book isn't to discourage you. It's to get real.

If you're writing for an indie budget, it means you'll need "other people's money." I've personally had several projects optioned and even had one greenlit up to $5 million. When you get news that a name actor bit on your script, life is awesome! Only later comes the cold morning light.

Other people's money equals loss of control. By definition the process becomes passive. You, as the writer, are perpetually waiting to hear back. Days turn into weeks, which turn into months. The trail gets hot, goes cold, and producers (for whatever reason) start considering other projects. You follow up leads, press hard, receive rejection, but you keep going. You don't take no for an answer. Then five years have gone by. The project isn't dead, but it isn't alive either. It's in development hell, a sort of limbo, someplace other than made.

Placements in screenwriting contests that lead nowhere — Pitchfest contests, cards exchanged, handshakes made, six months later zero happens; consultant feedback taken and rewrites done, sending it out again and *nothing* happens. I've been there, but I have never given up.

Again, I am not trying to dissuade you from writing movies with an indie budget. But when you write for this level, when it comes time to try to sell it, you will be taking on the indie landscape and all its permutations.

1.3 Micro-budget movies

Make no mistake, the micro-budget movie path will not be an easy road either. Everyone is making these movies, and this is probably the category you will be in when you are starting out as a filmmaker.

Have you see the submission numbers for the Sundance Film Festival? In 2013, there were 12,000-plus submissions! Here's a snippet from the Festival Director, John Cooper, in an interview about the 2013 Submission Process: "To me, it says that independent film is thriving. It's certainly exciting for us to receive 12,000 submissions this year for the first time ever, but more than that, we were really pleased by the overall quality of the films submitted to us. Each year the quality of independent film seems to rise, and we're chalking that up to this idea of a vital independent film community — directors, producers, DPs, and art directors all continuing to work in independent film throughout their careers and also well-known and really talented actors joining these projects."[2]

Out of 12,000 submissions, only 113 feature films were selected! If you run the numbers, the odds aren't great you're making it into

---

2 "John Cooper and Trevor Groth Dissect 2013 Sundance Film Festival," FILMCASTLive!, accessed February 2015. http://filmcastentertainment.blogspot.ca/2013/01/john-cooper-and-trevor-groth-dissect.html

Sundance with your micro-budget movie. However, there is something comforting in knowing that the barriers of entry have been lowered. The proactivity is enabling. There really is something you can do about making your dream happen. This is the promise of DIY filmmaking and the revolution for a filmmaking proletariat.

The beauty of the micro-budget movie is the control it gives you. What exactly is the budget for a micro-budget film? Similar to indies, there's no one-size-fits-all definition, but I'm comfortable saying that micro is any budget you can raise and control yourself. If it's within your power to raise $200,000, I'm calling that micro-budget. If you can only raise $10,000 but the movie gets made, it's micro-budget film.

Here's a great example of a micro-budget film: Tim Rutili, a friend of mine from Chicago, got into Sundance a couple of years ago with *All My Friends Are Funeral Singers*. It was a highly personal movie, which Rutili wanted to make a statement about superstition. What he didn't want to do, or even consider doing, is write a movie that would be sent to screenplay contests, readers, and agencies. He wanted to keep control of the process, saying exactly what he wanted, and make it for a price he could raise himself; thereby having to answer to no one but himself.

The film had a budget of $35,000 and no bankable stars. He beat the 12,000 to 1 odds because he wrote a script that was shot for $35,000, had a great soundtrack he provided himself with his band Califone, and an uncompromised vision that was truly original. Even though the film was accepted into Sundance, it didn't get a traditional distribution deal. However, it will make its money back and it has opened possible financial connections for his second movie. This DIY transformation was stoked by social media, the influx of cable markets seeking original content, and digital distribution options through video-on-demand platforms. Nowadays, writers and filmmakers have more options and a far greater freedom than even a decade ago.

Another example, is *Paranormal Activity*, by Oren Peli.This was Peli's first movie, and instead of using a traditional script, he used the technique of "retroscripting," which is a form of script that has a plot outline but leaves out the dialogue. This lets the actors improvise, which gives the characters more realistic dialogue.

It cost him $15,000 to make. He had few industry contacts, and no agent. In 2007, he screened the film at the Screamfest Horror Film Festival. It was a sensation. His actress won the Best Actress award. From this exposure, he got an agent. The movie was shown at Slamdance and again, it went over well.

By 2008 his little film was being shopped for distribution. A DVD made its way up the food chain at DreamWorks until it ended up with Steven Spielberg. DreamWorks producers purchased all domestic distribution for the movie for less than $1 million. They planned to reshoot the movie. Subsequent screenings blew enough people away that it was decided to release the director's original cut.

Squabbles between DreamWorks and Paramount delayed the film's release until 2009, but even this seemed to work in the film's favor. The initial release only went out to 12 college towns. Online audiences were encouraged to vote for an expanded release to 20 cities — large-market cities were excluded. By then, it went viral. Everyone had heard of this movie, but no one had seen it. A frenzy ensued for this $15,000 horror movie. *Paranormal Activity* was finally released multicity.

As of this writing it has grossed — wait for it — $107,917,283,[3] the single greater profiting movie.The sequel, *Paranomal Activity 2*, was a failure by comparison: It cost an outrageous $2,750,000 and has made a paltry $84,749,884!

What are the odds that your $20,000 credit card movie gets you a CAA Agent, a seven-figure sale, invites to Ouija board parties at Steven Spielberg's, or a Paranormal Activity 2-style sequel that grosses 84 mil?

Ah, not great. At all.

Does that mean this isn't a worthwhile approach? Of course not.

There are many success stories of micro-budget filmmakers:

- *The Blair Witch Project:* This film went viral before it even hit theaters.

- *El Mariachi:* This Robert Rodriguez film famously cost $7,000, and the film won multiple international awards.

- *Primer:* Shane Carruth's movie was also made with only $7,000, and the film won at the Sundance Film Festival in 2004.

- *Clerks:* This was Kevin Smith's first movie and he made it with $27,575. The film won the Filmmakers Trophy at the Sundance Film Festival, and was picked up by Miramax Films.

The key is that you must write your movie carefully, with an eye toward low-budget filmmaking, and with the intention of shooting

---

3 *Paranormal Activity* Total Grosses, Box Office Mojo, accessed February 2015.
  http://www.boxofficemojo.com/franchises/chart/?id=paranormalactivity.htm

it yourself. It must also stand apart from the many other low-budget movies out there. Filmmakers now have opportunities with the technological and marketplace innovations that have only just come into practice in the last few years.

There are tons of bad micro-budget movies made; perhaps more bad movies being made than ever before in history. However, a few of them will create a buzz.

If you're interested in exploring this path, you must have a clear vision about the movie you're writing, your target audience, and the marketplace. Once the "fun" of writing your movie is over, selling it becomes your mission.

2. To Live and Die in Los Angeles

There's no simplistic answer to what is, clearly, a complex and personal question when it comes to whether or not you move to Los Angeles.

Let's first consider the history of cinema in Chicago 1915. About 100 years ago, nearly 20 percent of all movies came from Chicago. The Essanay Film Manufacturing Company of Chicago, along with the Selig Polyscope Company, represented two of the top ten producers of silent films. Why Chicago didn't maintain that elite status had as much to do with the weather as it did with more complex issues, such as the burgeoning "film star system." The brutal Chicago winter of 1915 drove Charlie Chaplin out of town (he made only one film in Chicago for Essanay, *His New Job*), leaving along with the likes of Gloria Swanson (an extra at Essanay) and Bronco Billy Anderson (the first silent movie cowboy star) for the promise of year-round Los Angeles production and warm weather.

Flash forward to 2015 and you'll see Chicago has a thriving film community. There are a multitude of resources — student and professional — dedicated to making movies. Columbia College, DePaul University, and Tribeca Flashpoint Academy train hundreds of students to take a place in the film business every year. Chicago Filmmakers has been a grassroots film community for more than 20 years. The Illinois Film Office has been instrumental in drumming up production (31 percent tax giveback, one of the best of any state). Informal groups such as Chicago Screenwriters Network and Meetup.com nurture their own filmmaking communities.

There have been many movies filmed in Chicago over the years; here's a few of them:

- *The Dark Knight*
- *Batman Begins*
- *The Blues Brothers*
- *Sixteen Candles*
- *The Fugitive*

The resources Chicago brings as a superb filmmaking town are second to none. Everything, you could want is here except for the money — homegrown, major indie, feature-film production money.

Aside from the documentary company Kartemquin Films (*Hoop Dreams, Stevie*) and the occasional independent project produced by Jean "Gigi" Pritzker (*Green Street Hooligans*), where is the money coming from for indie-budgeted film production in Chicago? Los Angeles.

Which brings us back to you and the decision you need to make. Do you need to be in LA to be serious about your screenwriting career? There are so many factors to consider — age, family, job, and temperament. How long will you devote to giving filmmaking a shot as a career? Can you give it a year without success? Five years? What's realistic? Do you have the resources? Will you fit in with the LA lifestyle celebrated in everything from *Entourage* to *The Day of the Locust*? Are you ready for the sharks, schmoozers, and dream weavers?

I think there are a few things we can agree on:

- It'll be difficult to get hired to the writing staff for *Orange Is the New Black* if you live in Alabama.
- It'll be more difficult to take agent meetings at William Morris Endeavour if you live in Iowa.
- It'll be a long shot to work on the Paramount lot if you live in Rhode Island.
- It'll take a papal miracle to work a day gig as a production assistant if you live in Idaho.

It is truly about "who you know" and getting your script into the right hands. As we'll talk about later, this business is about relationships. It takes talent and a small bit of luck, but you have to work to build the connections you'll need.

A student had nothing happening in Chicago and so had nothing to lose by moving to LA. By hanging out with a friend who was going through a prestigious digital photography program, he met a producer and was attached to write a $1 million indie. He's currently writing his second film, working by day on film sets and meeting people he never would have in Chicago. Five years from now this guy could be a force in the industry, but it wouldn't happen if they were still living in Chicago.

That said, there are plenty of professionals who don't live in LA. At the beginning of your career, to a certain degree, you are your script. It doesn't matter if you're in LA or Chicago or Boise. If you write a red-hot spec script, it will find an audience.

3. Do You Need to Go to Film School?

When I was making my first movie, Jane Doe, I had no previous experience of being on a film set and so, I made all kinds of mistakes (see section 5.). I remember being handed Sidney Lumet's book, *Making Movies*, by one of our producers. "Maybe this'll help," he said delicately.

Had I been to film school, I might have had a clue in terms of film set responsibilities. This is the stuff of freshmen learning at Columbia College's Cinema Art + Science department. Thing is, you don't want to be on the set of a quarter-million-dollar film doing things on the fly. So let's say that yes, there's a place for film school, despite all the negativity you'll hear in certain quarters.

If I'd had formal training the chances of my first movie failing would have been reduced significantly. It's at least worth looking into adult education courses such as scriptwriting, supervision, producing, editing, and directing.

It's better to be a Jack of four employable filmmaking trades than an Ace of one. Whilst you're waiting to become Christopher Nolan or Quentin Tarantino, you might find that the third or fourth skill you learned in film school is the one with which you'll actually make a living — be it as a script supervisor, or digital image technician, or a casting agent, or a grip/gaffer. Learn as much as possible about the craft of making movies because your skills will help pay the bills while you struggle with the opportunities of being the writer.

4. When Should You Give up on a Screenplay?

Consider the bigger picture: You want your movie made. Aside from getting paid, have you figured out why you want to make it? You might want to examine your reasons. Is it the chase for legacy, for your name to live on 100 years from now? Or is it that you wanted to do good work that matters to others? Are you doing it for your life to have some context or meaning? Examine why is it you write in the first place; this might help you on your journey.

You've been working on this script for weeks, months, or maybe even years. You do what the experts recommend: Gather critiques, rewrite, send it out, deal with rejection, do more rewriting, send it out again, and deal with more rejection. It's sitting there on your computer and you know you need to make changes but it's reached the point where you can't even look at it! You are utterly and totally exhausted! And not one scintilla closer to getting it made. You are feeling crushed.

You've joined the Writers Guild of America (WGA), and you've graduated from Columbia's Cinema Art + Science program. Your parents have written checks to help you get through school and to launch your successful career, but nothing is happening.

You want to hang it up. Not just the one script, but maybe the whole mess. How many screenwriters actually make a living at it anyhow? You tried, you really did. You bang away at the front door of the "Hollywood Country Club" but nobody takes notice.

You've heard back from the world at large through screenwriting contests, query letters, manager inquiries, and their responses are rejections. Cryptic reader notes, generic rejection slips from boutique agencies, and no response at all from the bigwigs. The sound of Hollywood rejection is silence.

Or, maybe you've done OK. You've pitched a concept at Pitchfest and got some response from a junior agent. You've given it to friends and got excellent feedback, ran it through your screenwriting group, vetted and rewrote, sent it out again, and made the finalist round at a screenwriting competition, all of which has lead you nowhere.

As the years pass, you wonder if it is worth it. How can you know? If I've depressed you so far, let me just say this: Contrary to what the Hollywood gatekeepers will tell you, your time does have value. And here's another tidbit: There are some things you can control.

Overly simplistic as it might be, there are other paths besides beating your head to a bloody pulp against Hollywood's front door.

I've had excellent students who worked for months on a script, submitted it to Academy Nicholl Screenwriting Competition but they didn't make it past the first round. Unfortunately, some never recovered from the rejection. Consider these two points:

1. If you pack in your writing that quickly after a single rejection, it might be for the best. Screenwriting demands discipline. You will be critiqued and you will rewrite, perpetually, endlessly, and not always be paid for your efforts. Unless you're writing the check to make the movie, you don't get to decide when the script is done.

2. What strikes me as delusional, or downright absurd, is that you would let some person you've never met, whose qualifications cannot be verified (e.g., a screenplay contest reader, an agent's assistant, a manager recently graduated from college) pronounce judgment over whether the script you just worked eight months on is good or bad. What does that mean? Purely subjective opinion, end of story. Why would you let a single person, or even a hundred people, stop you?

Don't give up. Instead, think about alternatives to the front door of the Hollywood Country Club. You want in, period. Is there a back door to the joint that will help you find your way in? More than likely, there is.

If you want to pack up your script, or even your attempt at a career as a filmmaker, do it. No one but you should decide that. Put the script on the shelf and let it sit there. Come back to it later, or never come back to it. The decision is yours. If you want it bad enough, don't ever let anyone tell you no.

5. How a Casino Dice Dealer Wrote a Movie That Ended up in Every Video Store in North America ... in An Age of Such Things As Video Stores

What is the difference in trying to write a $250,000 Calista Flockhart vehicle shot on Super 16 mm versus writing for "no-name" Chicago actors with a $44,000 budget? What are the challenges of going from a culture of indie-filmmaking to digital DIY in terms of the scriptwriting process?

Let's start by looking at *Jane Doe* and how it got made. We'll also look at how it ended up at every video rental store in the country, making a couple million bucks along the way. Take note of the life lessons in this section and learn from our mistakes.

The genesis of *Jane Doe* starts with the name. I am a sucker for long titles. How about this one: *A Fire Was Burning over the Dumpling House One Chinese New Year.* That's a tough one for a movie marquee, but it works fine for a play title. *Dumpling House* was a play I wrote about Claire G, a heroin-addict and my girlfriend, back in New York circa 1983.

It won't spoil a 30-year-old play and 15-year-old movie to tell you things didn't turn out well for her. I wrote the play two days after we buried her. I wrote it in four days. Three months later it was being performed in Chicago at IgLoo, the Theatrical Company. This was a company formed by my brother Chris and his then-wife Maria. They took on the lead roles and the play, appropriately for our micro-budget purposes, was put up for the price of a couple pizzas. Costumes were made from scratch or found in dumpsters. Sets were created with scraps of wood found in dumpsters, a mattress on the floor, a beat-down table and chairs. It was my first play and the company's second; it created a buzz.

The way to break through into the consciousness of people is to take a personal story and turn it into the universal. That process of transmutation is called writing. When what resonates for you, personally, resonates for someone in the dark of the theater, you're on the right path. The play was about addiction. Addiction has been done in both theater and film. However, what about the point of view of the person living with the addict? I didn't even know the term "enabler" then, but what about showing the cost of addiction, the hell and insanity of it, the not knowing what to do. There are many people with substance abuse problems so this one hit close to home. Of every ten folks who saw the play, five were in tears when the lights came up.

It ran for months in Chicago; then it followed Chris and Maria to Los Angeles for a production there. Then back to Chicago for a return run, ending sometime in 1988. And then it sat for seven years.

Unpublished, no other theatrical performance was done with it. It wasn't until I started writing screenplays in 1995 that I adapted it for film. My brother had also shifted to movies and championed Dumpling House (retitled *Pictures of Baby Jane Doe*). I was working on a casino boat and wrote it gloriously ignorant of all things screenwriting. I didn't concern myself one iota with mundane aspects such as the budget. Dedicated to Claire G, it had to be shot in New York and Atlantic City.

I continued dealing dice in Aurora, Illinois, leaving the trivial details of fund-raising to my producer brother who swore a blood oath to make it happen. But the question was, how can we make it happen? We began by asking for money from people we knew. Dad, being a documentary filmmaker himself, started the ball rolling, pumping in the first money. (Hey Dad, you rule!) Mom happened to run one of the top vintage stores in New York City and offered to fully costume the actors plus use her store for a location, and she gave us some cash too. (Hey Mom, you're a giver!)

We had raised $90,000 so Chris worked to make the movie under a Screen Actors Guild (SAG) Limited X contract. I was just the craps dealer/writer back then and didn't question his figures when he announced we could do it, with the script *as is*. We set out with the full intention to shoot it for $90,000, until Unapix Entertainment entered the picture.

5.1 Know who you're getting into bed with!

Unapix Entertainment was a video distributor whose credits included *Judy Tenuta: Un-Butt Plugged in Tex-Ass!, Jack Frost 2: Revenge of the Killer Mutant Snowman*, and the underrated *My Brother the Pig*. With a track record like that, little wonder they went under in 2001. Of course in 1995 we didn't know we were getting into bed with hacks.

My brother and I were summoned to the offices of Unapix Entertainment, which was in midtown Manhattan, a Park Avenue address. Escorted into the President's office and sat down in a pair of $500 chairs. The President sat behind his fancy Gorman desk and proceeded to tell us how tremendously impressed he was with the script.

"A very moving story," he said, and then asked, "Did it move you when you wrote it?"

"Well, my girlfriend died, so ... you know ... " Yes indeed, powerful stuff; thus, the reason for this meeting.

He wanted in. He knew we had prepped for a $90,000 ultra-low-budget shoot but how about if Unapix came in and helped? He then slid a check across the table made out for $150,000 dollars! It's quite something to stare at a $150,000 check that someone wants to give you. How many of you would have the intestinal fortitude to push it away?

There were handshakes all around, and the assurance that the paperwork would be sent over in the morning. True to the President's word, the next day the contract arrived and it was about the size of a phonebook. We hired a young lawyer, who was a friend of my brother, to help us interpret the document.

5.2 Hire the best entertainment lawyer you can possibly afford

Our guy was good in pointing out the obvious: Boilerplate language lead to two major points:

1. Unapix owned all domestic distribution.

2. Unapix would control the final cut. This meant that while I, as the director, would edit to the rough cut, Unapix would have final say on the final cut. Unapix controlled the movie in its final form.

Unapix would also receive first monies to pay back its investment plus profit percentages.

What did I know? I was a craps dealer living in a subbasement apartment in Aurora, Illinois. The business end bored me to tears. I just wanted to shoot a movie that honored my dead girlfriend.

I recall some discussion of the boilerplate language. Could we trust them? Well, the meeting with the President couldn't have gone better. They respected our artistic instincts. We wouldn't have a problem on the back end.

5.3 Trust your instincts with casting

Next we had a meeting with the project's producer and point woman for the Unapix interests (we'll call her Niki, which is not her real name). First impressions were mutually impressive. I noticed the Tony Award on Niki's desk for a play she produced on Broadway. From our dumpster diving non-equity Chicago theater days, we had definitely taken a step up in class. Chris and I sat before her and listened as she gushed on about our abilities, saying we were the "new Coen Brothers" and our "futures were bright, bright, bright!"

With the Unapix money we moved up in class to SAG low-budget status. We were able to make better offers to the agencies and some amazing actors rolled into our auditions. The bigger name actors wouldn't audition for us; they wanted offers presented to them.

While name actors will open doors in terms of festivals and distribution, the lesser-named actors with passion might give far better performances. Remember that you'll be spending up to 12 hours a day on set with him or her. Who would you rather spend three weeks of 12-hour days with? Gather opinions from your inner circle, but trust your gut.

While finding the supporting players was challenging, nothing compared to casting the main character's role of Jane. Never had that level of actress competed to read my words, but none of them made the top two. Lara Phillips, who had won the Joseph Jefferson Award for Nelson Algren's Never Come Morning, was my choice. She had range, from innocence to devastating depth. She'd be totally believable as a junky. I flew her in for the audition thinking, "I'm the writer and director — I get to decide who plays the lead role." Wrong!

Another actress entered the discussion. She had done a small speaking part in the movie Quiz Show but nothing much in film. Her bigger accomplishments were in theater. In 1994 she debuted on Broadway as Laura in The Glass Menagerie. She had glowing reviews, star-in-the-making kind of stuff. When Gersh Agency sent her over she was not famous in any way. In walked Calista Flockhart.

As to the matter of talent, whatever that "it-factor" was, Calista had it. This led to a tough call. Chris, the producer and lead actor, wanted Calista. I was sticking with Lara. I had a working relationship with her, knew what she was capable of, and damn it, I was the director! Chris wasn't backing off, so we were deadlocked. I remember three days of pure warfare, the two of us going back and forth. If he was to act in this movie, he had to have chemistry with the actress playing Jane. He had it with Calista and didn't with Lara.

The solution was to take it out of our hands and give it to an inner circle of producers, those who knew the project best. Audition tapes were distributed to five people — 48 hours later, the results were in: Calista would be Jane.

If we look at any single reason why Jane Doe landed four boxes across at every video store in the country, it's found right here: Cast well. When given a choice, always choose the actress who will become nationally famous within ten months. Had we known that inside a year Calista would become the star of Ally McBeal, or that three years later she'd be on the cover of TIME magazine, we might have done things a bit differently. Maybe we would have told Unapix that we were passing on its offer, and slide that $150,000 check back to the President. Maybe we would have kept domestic distribution, and found the money for pick-up photography, reshoot some of the 20 scenes that we didn't have time to shoot the first time around, reshape the fine cut with all new design elements and a fully re-edited version according to our vision.

5.4 There's no such thing as a do-over

I used to begin the Columbia College classes I teach showing the video of my brother appearing on *Entertainment Tonight* and *Access Hollywood*. When *Jane Doe* came out we were besieged. Ally McBeal as a junky? Calista as you've never seen her before!

I remember walking into video stores. In New York for Christmas, there's *Jane Doe* at a video store on 14th Street and Union Square. Shopping in Times Square? There it was at a Hollywood Video store on 44th Street. Friends called me from Seattle and Portland, seeing the movie for sale there. It was all over Chicago, in Wisconsin … we even had reports of an appearance in Atlantic City. This for a movie without a theatrical release, with no reviews, that appeared at exactly *one* film festival (which it won).

Unapix Entertainment went bankrupt in 2001. We never did get a full reporting on dollar figures. The public figure it disclosed for sales of the movie was a little more than $1 million. Knowing the crafty accounting standards of distributors in general, and how trustworthy our bankrupt partners were, especially where it came to profit sharing with us, one might assume more money flowed in from the movie. We'll never know, but we have only ourselves to blame.

The beauty about taking a beat down from life is that you can make a conscious decision to never let that happen again. I won't guarantee that it doesn't, but take it from a former craps dealer, the mathematical possibilities diminish. It's better to have lived it, learned from it, and moved on.

5.5 When hiring a director, choose one who has actually been on a movie set

Those who read my blog at Script Gods Must Die know that the kicker to the *Jane Doe* story is that I directed the movie in the first place. Try to get your arms around this one: I had never directed a movie before. Fact is, I had never stepped foot on a movie set.

How exactly do you hire a director with zero experience? Ask the brain trust — my brother Chris, Producer, and my father, the Executive Producer. The thinking might have gone like this: Paul wrote it. Hell,

Paul lived it! Nobody knows the world like him. Nobody knows Atlantic City or the meat market district of New York (where we were shooting) like him. Nobody could be more passionate. Give him a shot!

All true. I had total dedication to the memory of my girlfriend. This movie would come as close as possible to how we actually lived it, and the tragedy of how it actually ended. Note that noble sentiments are guaranteed to doom your project. As it did with *Jane Doe*.

5.6 Don't direct the movie of your life

"Paul, this isn't a documentary, it's a feature film." If only someone had whispered those words in my ear. Passion is fine, but when it comes time to make your movie, to be fully in control of the movie-making mechanism, to be a leader to the cast and crew, to have the long view, the overview, the objectivity you need, I'm here to tell you, DISpassion is more important.

Just because it happened to you, doesn't make it interesting. Just because it happened to you, doesn't make it a movie. Sure, you want to draw on your real life as a writer. Write what you know, all those cobwebbed clichés. You've got to find the personal truth that resonates with people. However, that doesn't mean it should be an A-to-Z, step-by-step re-creation of what actually happened.

Nobody cares if you actually worked at the German buffet where a three-month-old slice of strudel caused Mr. Moustache to have a heart attack! Nobody cares if the seagull actually crapped on your head while you were talking to Grandmama! Nobody cares if your girlfriend actually died of a drug overdose. It's not a documentary, it's a movie. All people care about and all you owe the audience, is a good story.

Avoid choosing locations not because they were the best choice, but because of personal history. The audience will never know that you and your girlfriend argued outside that bar, or that you actually ate at that Mexican restaurant. I was guilty of doing this stuff, such as the night before our first day of production, sleeping in the former rooming house where I lived with Claire, to "get into the spirit of it."

I remember being questioned by Calista at one point, the script called for her to stash drugs in a hidden pullout ceiling panel. She said it didn't seem likely, that she'd never do that, and that an audience might not buy it. I said, "But that's how Claire did it. It happened." Wrong! Nobody cares if it happened, dummy! This is a movie. The only question should be: Will an audience buy it?

The detachment required of a director will not be found in the person who wrote the movie.

Here's a message to you, Dear Reader, infuse your words with passion and originality. Put the audience into the heads of your characters. Trap them in there with all the good and bad decisions, all the darkness and light. Then step off, and step back. Let someone else direct the movie of your life.

I leave *Jane Doe* to places like Pirate Bay who saved it from total obscurity with that Swedish subtitled torrent. Oh sure, it can still be found online, or bought at Amazon. I make not a penny on these, and haven't in years. And that's OK. In truth, I've made my peace with it. For your purposes, do as I say, not as I did.

Can we rework this, please.

As a postscript: *Jane Doe* is still out there. You can rent it on Netflix, buy it on Amazon, or steal it on Pirate Bay. God bless that one seeder in Sweden, keeping my little movie alive!

I won't make a penny on any of these. And that is fine. In truth, I've moved on from *Jane Doe*. But for your purposes, Good Reader, do as I say, not as I did.

Working As a Director
(It's All about Relationships)

A film set is the most fascinating environment I've ever worked on, and one of my favorite places to be. It's a strange mix of creativity, spontaneity, but also hopefully stringent organization. It's a place where dozens, sometimes hundreds of people come together to bring a creation together, each with their very specific role.

If you are the director, you are the link that holds the entire chain together, and likely the only person who has a complete vision of what is going on. You've worked with the production designer to create the look and feel of the sets, with the director of photography to compose your shots, with your assistant director to schedule them and organize them, with your actors to rehearse the scenes, and with all the other key crewmembers to make sure each person that walks onto the set knows exactly what they will be doing during the time that is allotted to each day. You have ultimate decision-making power on all aspects — and since with great power comes great responsibility, you also have the ultimate responsibility to your producer and financiers to ensure that each day gets completed as timely as possible and within the allotted budget.

If you've done your job properly in preproduction, everything should be planned and timed to the minute; theoretically, you shouldn't even need to be there. However, once you step on a live set, everything changes. Unexpected problems arise, delays accumulate, and it's your job to make the right decisions to ensure that you come out with a complete film.

An independent film set is also probably one of the most stressful work environments you'll ever find. As opposed to large productions you do not have the luxury of picking up scenes the next day and you have to make it fit. You also need to maintain morale through tough days, with a crew that will likely become more and more exhausted as time goes by. This is why it is essential that you have good relationships with your key people, as you will be relying on these relationships to trickle down to the rest of the crew and to carry you through the inevitable tough times that will arise throughout the shoot. This is why the best way I can think of breaking down a shoot is through these relationships.

1. The First Assistant Director (AD)

The first assistant director (AD) is your right arm and the extension of yourself on set. He or she is responsible for organizing the set, and is the master of the set on a day-to-day basis. The AD is also responsible for keeping the clock, informing you when you go overtime, and making sure the day is completed as scheduled. Any good first AD is constantly looking at his or her watch and hollering out every few minutes: "Five minutes to first shot on the next scene!" "Five-minute break!" "Three minutes before we need to move on!"

Your first AD should know the schedule and shot list for the day pretty much by heart, and is there to guide you and put you back on track when you get lost in creative discussions or any other time-consuming deviations from the plan. The person needs to be able to help you make choices such as advise on shots that should or could be cut if you're running out of time. He or she is there to convey your requests to the key crewmembers, and make sure everyone understands where the day is at and what's next to come.

From a human standpoint, being a first AD is also the most challenging job on set. His or her role combines the good cop and the bad cop because the AD has to enforce time and rules, yet convey encouragement to the crew and resolve human conflicts as they arise.

On *Roundabout American* I had a fantastic AD, Angie Gaffney, a 19-year-old sophomore student who, three years later, now runs her own production company. Angie understood the entire filmmaking process, was extremely organized, and had all the right people skills. Without her it is unlikely the film would ever have been completed. This being my first feature as a director I was still finding my marks, and Angie was able to offer insight and run the crew with little to no assistance from me, which was great. Yet even she found herself crossing boundaries a couple times with the lines being so fine between keeping the shoot under control and being too hard on people. I'll always remember the time where she screamed into her microphone to her second AD who had just injured his leg the day before "Don't walk — run!" She was effectively doing her job by trying to catch up on lost time but had momentarily lost track of the human component, which is even more essential — the second you risk demotivating people you compromise the entire shoot.

The assistant director's role often also consists of mediating between the director and crewmembers when things get tense. No matter how hard you try, the tension on a set will try even the strongest relationships and will break weak ones. On every shoot I've ran, I have ended up at one point or another in conflict with at least one key crewmember — this is where the AD can step in as an impartial mediator and hopefully minimize friction.

2. The Director of Photography (DP)

The relationship between a director of photography (DP) and a director can be almost symbiotic, and many pairs work together for years on project after project. This has been the case for me; I've worked with the same DP, Fred Miller, on almost all my films. The DP is your eyes on set and the person who crafts the visuals you have in mind to match the director's vision as closely as possible. On smaller independent films in particular, where storyboards are almost nonexistent, it is absolutely crucial to work with someone who understands your thinking process and to whom you can convey your thoughts in an effective yet economical manner. If it takes your DP four rounds of adjustments to produce a minor change, you're probably not working together very efficiently.

On an independent shoot, the DP is likely the person you will be spending the most time with. Fred and I always joke about the number of hours we have spent cramped together in tiny spaces joined to the hip like Siamese twins. We've gotten used to each other enough to speak briefly and frankly without mincing words. If I think one of the shots he's setting up is not up to par, I can tell him without being afraid of hurting his feelings, and conversely he's told me bluntly when he thought I was making the wrong call on set and was right more often than not.

I usually go through a number of prep sessions with Fred prior to a shoot, and we come up with a shot list where we discuss each scene, all the setups and shots that are needed, etc. We then convey this to the AD and have a couple meetings so he or she fully understand the structure.

Unfortunately for the AD (and this is not a practice I recommend, but it's the result of two people working together too much with limited resources), Fred and I have a tendency to then step on set, and drastically modify the shot list on the fly, which causes confusion. Things tend to change when you actually see them — days run long and some scenes need to be cut or can be simplified. This is where having an AD that fully understands the process is essential, as he or she can then modify the shot list on the fly and convey the changes to the rest of the crew (not to mention advise on changes that seem like they could save time initially, but actually end up complicating the day).

Once the preliminary run-through is done for a given scene, Fred gets to work with his crew to set up lights and first shot. This is when you realize that no one works as much as the DP on an independent film. While Fred sets up, I get to have a break, and everyone else is waiting or prepping. Then, when we go to shoot, most of his lighting crew is standing by for minor adjustments. However, the DP is active through virtually every minute of every day of shooting, which is a remarkable feat.

On bigger sets this is not the case as the DP tends to have all his or her lighting setups preplanned and can just have the gaffer and the crew set up for the next shot while he or she takes a break. On micro-budget films, the DP is by far the hardest working person on set, and one of the most important.

3. The Script Supervisor

A role often neglected or left to hire for the last minute, the script supervisor is actually the third most important person for a director to lean on after the AD and DP. The script supervisor's role is threefold:

1. Make sure everything in the script and shot list is captured, and is to spec (meaning the lines actually match the script).

2. Make sure everything is properly labeled and prepped for post-production (that slates match scene numbers, that shots are properly numbered and logged, getting details on which takes are good or bad for the editor, etc.).

3. Make sure that continuity is respected (i.e., that a character does the same hand movement with the same hand in consecutive shots or takes, that from one shot to the other sets, costumes and makeup are consistent, and that generally everything makes sense). For example, "Would this individual with a strong aversion to light really sit in this sunbathed booth without his glasses?"

It is a critical task, and as easy as it may seem at first glance it requires incredible skill and attention to detail. I've worked with both excellent and terrible script supervisors, and even though you can make a film with someone mediocre in that position, having a good script supervisor on set makes the process much smoother.

The script supervisor will constantly be standing by the director and camera. His or her tools are a timer, a digital camera, and a notepad. They photograph everything, time everything, and write it down. A good script supervisor will know to be unobtrusive, as he or she stands right in the midst of people in charge of the creative decisions, yet also knows to speak up when he or she sees something wrong. It's someone you might forget is there, but who you'll dearly miss if he or she is not present.

4. The Producer

The producer's job, and the job of his or her representatives (i.e., the line producer or production manager), is to ensure that all the needs are met for the director and creative crew to complete the film, and to ensure that it is all done within budget.

The producer's job is not to inquisitively monitor the director, make creative suggestions (or worse, decisions), or to in any other way try to influence the creative work (other than by expressing budgetary or timing constraints if they are legitimate and seem unnoticed by the rest of the crew). In other words, the producer should act on set as a facilitator, not a controller. I've been lucky enough to work almost exclusively with producers who understood this and were very respectful. I would recommend having this conversation ahead of time to make sure the roles are clearly defined; otherwise, it can lead to major conflict and an unhealthy atmosphere.

5. The Production Designer

The production designer and the art crew are responsible for crafting the set and providing for all design and set-related needs during the shoot.

When hiring production designers, people often look at the portfolio and creative abilities of the individual. While this is indeed one of the primary elements to consider for the position, it is very important to also keep in mind that on smaller shoots the production designer will likely be responsible for handling his or her department on set with the help of a junior art director, and that he or she is also responsible for one of the larger portions of the budget and for a substantial portion of crew. This implies that you need individuals that beyond being creative are also extremely responsible, efficient, and who understand crew etiquette.

One of my pet peeves with art department people are the ones who consider their job done once a set is put together, and forget that adjustments and resets are constantly required while shooting a scene and that it is crucial to have an art department member dedicated to have his or her eye on the monitor at all times, ready to jump when a scene is over to reset or adjust as needed.

6. The Hair and Makeup Artists

The role of the hair and makeup artists goes way beyond hair and makeup. They are the casts' confidants, and having a good relationship with them can inform you of potential problems with the cast before they occur and help avert crises. Because of the time they spend with each cast member, they tend to befriend them quickly and have a much better feel for their stress levels and sources of frustration than any other crewmember.

Many times my hair and makeup person was the one to inform me that a cast member was frustrated with a crewmember or with me, or that he or she was apprehensive about an upcoming scene, giving the opportunity to address the issues before they became explosive.

7. The Sound Engineer

On smaller shoots the audio department usually consist of one or two people. It can be difficult to find solid people at low cost, and it's worth spending more if available to get professionals.

Their job tends to be seamless and technical, but is absolutely essential to the film. On set good sound people are quiet and efficient, they know to make themselves unobtrusive, and they understand the camera well enough to know how to avoid interfering with shots.

8. The Talent

I could write an entire chapter on the relationship between director and cast. It is complex, and the nature of that relationship can impact the film like none other. Every director works differently so I can only speak to my approach.

I tend to think of cast members as highly skilled artists who carry the highest amount of pressure on set. Everyone else can screw up and it will likely get unnoticed, but if a cast member screws up, the entire crew is there to see it. If that same cast member screws up a second time, he or she is likely to start losing confidence, screw up again, become more aware of the crew watching them, the problem snowballing, and then you have a problem.

I am a believer in rehearsal. The more you rehearse the better off you are. While everyone doesn't share this opinion — some directors claiming it kills spontaneity — I believe that trained and professional film actors know how to recreate spontaneity on every delivery, and rely on practice to find that spontaneity.

A film actor has to take into account new parameters and variables on set (e.g., camera placement, markers, requirements linked to depth of field and frame). In order for the actor to be able to process these elements while focusing on his or her delivery, he or she needs to have that delivery be second nature prior to the shoot.

The most essential element on set is to spare your actors and make them work as little as possible, which means having them do the bulk of their artistic work before the shoot. Because shooting days can be long, actors at the end of a 12-hour day don't have the basic luxury everyone else has of looking tired. So, the more rest they get the better. Minimize their time on the set, if possible. Use stand-ins, and always work with the AD to schedule things so the actors don't have to be present if they are not necessary.

The keyword is trust. As much as you rely tremendously on every crewmember, trust defines the actor-director relationship. Building trust prior to the shoot is essential. This is the reason many directors tend to recast actors. Establish trust and familiarity, like a shorthand between you. The actor needs to have faith in you, believe that if you ask him or her to do something, it is for good reason, and also believe that your feedback to him or her will be sincere — that you will not shy away from respectfully pointing at takes that are less than what they could be.

Actors get little feedback. They don't see the monitor (most hate watching themselves no matter what) and are surrounded by people who are afraid of being honest with them. Your job as the director is to give them honest feedback while preserving their self-confidence — a line that can be tricky to navigate.

Conversely you need to trust your cast to make choices and to pull through. Every actor will have that one scene where he or she just can't get it right take after take, and where the crew gets irritated with him or her. It is your job as the director make the actor feel trusted, and to give him or her confidence to get that one perfect take. You're the person the actor relies on so don't let him or her down.

9. Writer on Set

My only experience with a writer on set was with Paul on *Chat*. The most vivid memory I have was the day we were shooting in a clinic and during hour 11, I stumbled across him entertaining the production team by playing with a pair of plastic breast implants. Now, to be clear, in no way am I implying that Paul was not behaving properly as the writer on set. Quite the opposite — he was doing (and always did) his job perfectly — primarily there to observe and keep out of the way.

I've heard horror stories of a writer who comes on set, realizes that things are so different from what he or she imagined when writing the script, and start firing off artistic suggestions to the director and department heads. For example, "Don't you think Bob's car should be blue? I really saw it as powder blue when I was writing the script ... powder ... blue."

That is a nightmare and one of the reasons not to have the writer on set unless you know the person is aware of set etiquette or you think you will really need him or her (e.g., you foresee last-minute dialogue changes due to time or location switches).

Despite my apprehension at having Paul on set, I would gladly have him show up on the next film we make. Not only was he quiet, he regularly volunteered as "coffee bitch" (going out on coffee runs for myself and Fred when no production assistants were available). He also doubled as the on-set photographer and documented the whole shoot.

Micro-Budget Screenwriting: What to Consider before You Write Your Movie

> "The ideal low-budget movie is set in the present, with few sets, lots of interiors, only a couple speaking actors (none of them known), no major optional effects, no horses to feed. It's no wonder so many beginning movie-makers set a bunch of not-yet-in-the-Guild teenagers loose in an old house and have some guy in a hockey mask go around and skewer them."
>
> — John Sayles, Thinking in Pictures

Know yourself and your project. By ignoring the budget while writing your screenplay you guarantee needing other people's money. This guarantees the need of LA and the necessity of the LA mechanism. Writing your spec script, if you feel you need $100 million to tell the tale, go ahead and write it. But understand that the list of people who can actually make your flick just got narrowed by the necessity to find

$100 million. Needing other people's money, by definition, cedes power to them. It's why you should consider writing with a budget in mind.

There's no definition for what micro-budget is. If I'm reaching for a definition, a micro-budget is whatever funding you can pull from your pocket, or the pockets of your family, or the pockets of every friend you ever had when you send the personal email begging for cash during your 30-day Kickstarter campaign. Micro-budget is money you directly control, without strings. If you've raised, or can raise, $25,000, you better write your movie with that figure in mind.

1. Top Ten Considerations

Here are my top eight things to consider as you sit down to write your micro-budget:

1. Limit locations.

2. Limit characters.

3. Kids, Weather, Animals, Blood, and FX Effects= Just Don't Write 'Em!

4. Write longer dialogue scenes.

5. Limit the page count.

6. Beware of overreliance on postproduction digital solutions (e.g., fixing it in postproduction).

7. Avoid exterior shots.

8. Avoid special prop or makeup needs.

Conceive a movie that can be made on micro-budget. Outline it. Write the first draft. Get notes from your inner circle and rewrite it. Repeat the process until the script is ready to be shot on the budget you have raised.

How do you write a movie for the absolute lowest price possible without compromising the vision of the film? Let's expand on the points in the top ten list.

1.1 Limit locations

Job 1 for the micro-budget screenwriter is fashioning a story that limits production costs. One of the key production costs are locations.Ideally, as you write the micro-budget screenplay, you will write in only available resources. That means writing a location available to you free, or what you can get free.

Apartments, bars, and restaurants are commonly used. These are plentiful in most any city and can be found at little to no cost.

For our micro-budget film *Chat*, Boris managed to nail down the office he worked at to be our cybersex offices. Amusing juxtaposition, thinking of what was happening in those conference rooms from Monday through Friday, and then what nastiness we were up to from Friday night until early Monday morning when we finally stopped shooting our marathon weekends. The office location was worth at least $10,000 dollars (if we would have had to rent a similar space) and added tremendous production value. We shot 10 of the 18 production days and a pick-up day in the office.

Boris had initially budgeted $1,500 for the offices, and nothing for the apartment, thinking an apartment would be easy to find for free through friends and connections. The apartment ended up costing $1,000. That's because the apartment needed a certain look and feel — upscale yet dark and claustrophobic — and Boris had underestimated the difficulty of finding a space that combined both these criteria for free.

On an indie film you will often find yourself compromising on locations as a director will need to be extremely aware of what matters and what doesn't. Too many first-time directors end up eating more of their budget than necessary because they have their mind set on a certain look for a given location, which is something that will not usually be noticed by the audience. Always ask yourself what purpose a certain location is supposed to serve in the film, and if you have access to a space that could be suitable and is free or inexpensive, try to make it work, especially if it's a dialogue scene where the focus will likely be on the characters and not the surroundings.

One helpful trick when looking at permits for public spaces is to try to associate yourself with a student or faculty member from a film school. If you have such a person as one of your producers, you can usually get heavily discounted permits. In Chicago, for example, a permit to shoot in the parks goes down from $1,500 to $35.

You can also be smart and make one apartment appear like multiple locations. Someone volunteers his or her place? Great! You can shoot Character A's bathroom, Character B's kitchen, and Character C's living room all within the same apartment. This scheduling consolidating will be done by producers but it's your script they're locking in, so give them the best opportunity to make it happen within budget.

However, if you don't want a "claustrophobic's script," you will need to move the story to other locations. At the same time you want to limit those to, ideally, what you have access to for free. A liposuction doctor's office, as we found on *Chat*, is a bit harder to come across. This was a major discussion at the script stage: Did we absolutely need the liposuction office to tell the tale?

Understand that every new location you write equals a company move which equals more dollars spent. The producer has to pay the crew to pack equipment into company trucks and vans, drive to the new location, and unpack. You want to limit the necessity of company moves.

As long as you write only absolutely essential locations, producers can budget the strict minimum for location needs. We live in a world where so many films are made with such high budgets that viewers are used to seeing lavish locations in every film. You might think this implies that featuring generic locations will put your film at a disadvantage, but that's not the right way to look at it. The reality of DIY film is that the most expensive location you'll be able to afford will likely still be fairly small, and that nobody will remember it. In the end your actors and the story are what is making your film interesting — not where it takes place.

1.2 Limit characters

Even if the story you're writing is character-driven, it doesn't mean you'll need 10 principal and secondary characters to tell it. I would suggest limiting key characters to five or less. SAG minimum is $125 a day. Your producing team can't spend that on 10 actors and maintain a budget.

Force yourself to make sure every character has a purpose. Limit the number of extras and crowd scenes. Do not write in Wrigley Field, do not write in Union Station. Don't force producers to find a hundred extras unless there's no movie without them.

1.3 Kids, Weather, Animals, Blood, and FX Effects = Just Don't Write 'Em!

You're the writer. You think it's not your job to know that the simple gunplay you innocently wrote in will require a gun wrangler to oversee and train the actors. Or that it requires a Chicago Police Department officer on set for the full day. Or that Chicago cops get double-time if your shoot happens to stretch into 15 hours. Or that you need someone to convincingly mix blood and apply it to the actors. You didn't really think about all that when you wrote those two simple lines into the script because, well, you just didn't. These things you write have to be made to happen, and that costs $$$.

The question you have to ask is: Did they need to happen to tell the story and not compromise the movie's vision?

Kids are only allowed to work half a day on a film set, and the producer must pay for a child Welfare Officer or/and Teacher to be present at all times. Whenever you write a kid in your script, you are paying for an adult who will not appear on screen.

Writing in snow, wind, or rain is a bad idea. Where's the budget to build a rain gutter? How are you planning on designing snow that actually looks like snow when you've given your art department a $500 budget. You don't write about weather unless it's an absolute necessity to the story. For example, in *Chat*, the lead character (Falcon) has an aversion to light called photophobia. He can't take even moderate light. I made the mistake of writing in the last shot of the movie as a bright sunny day where he looks up into the sun, purposely. Well, that's great, except that the two days we shot there was minimal sunshine! Fortunately the sun peeked out for a half-hour stretch and we got the shot. But I should have never written that in in the first place.

With all due respect to the good people of PETA, I still have nightmares dealing with them on my movie, *Jane Doe*. I had written in a scene where our hero invites the girl he's enamored with over to tea. As he picks up a doughnut, a cockroach appears. Our hero takes a bite anyhow.

On set, it was a nightmare. These cockroaches weren't street bugs. They had to be imported–at a cost, and pinned down with PETA's consent–to get the shot. When the camera rolled, they were not cooperative at all! By the time we were finally ready to shoot I wondered why the f*&^ I wrote them in at all.

Note that PETA's consent is not required when using animal or bugs, it is only necessary to get the label "no animals were harmed in the making of this film." It's also a safeguard against any lawsuits related to animal treatment. Independent films almost never get PETA involved due to the complexity, but if you have animal-heavy scenes, you probably should consider it.

1.4 Write longer dialogue scenes

While there might be some downside to not having money for action stunts, the upside is it makes the writer utterly essential in the process of the micro-budget. People love great storytelling. They are starved for powerful and original work. Writing micro-budget means concentrating on the character-driven story, dialogue, and juxtaposition of things in your brain the world has never seen before. Think *Eraserhead* over *Tomb Raider* or *Happiness* over *Battleship*.

Dialogue scenes are less expensive to shoot because there are fewer camera and lighting set ups. You can shoot faster, and make your days more easily with heavy dialogue. You have a greater chance of shooting more pages per day as a result.

1.5 Limit the page count

You can't write a 105-page micro-budget. You want your final script to be less than 100 pages because every page costs money. Reduce the page count to the best of your ability. For your first draft, you can write with no limits and show your vision exactly as you see it. However, in your follow-up drafts reduce the page count.

When you get to the white production draft (also called shooting script), every scene should be boiled down to necessity (meaning, if you remove it, the story falls apart), and trimming every scene, and every line of action and dialogue, for necessity.

1.6 Beware of overreliance on postproduction digital solutions (fixing it in postproduction)

For my film *Jane Doe* we were regularly not making our days, meaning we weren't getting enough coverage of every shot. We tried to fix this in postproduction with editing cheats, for instance having an actor speak while the camera was on something or someone else. It looked false and really bad. Another example is that you can digitally place a muzzle flash into a plastic gun, but often everyone know it's fake and it looks bad. Choosing to do that versus using action guns and capturing the sound and look of gunfire in camera there's no comparison; do it real time and in camera.

1.7 Avoid exterior night shots

People think you don't have to light digital movies. This is an absolute fallacy. Some digital cameras require more lighting. And setting up outside is always a wild card. Also, your crowd control is dicey because you're a micro-budget and might only have a handful of friends or students to help out as production assistants. It's a constant battle to find people to work for free. Point being, you don't need crowd control in an already controlled interior setting.

For whatever purpose, I decided to give the biggest monologue of *Chat* to a one-scene character in an exterior night shot, which was difficult to shoot due to sound troubles. Here are some examples of the problems we had:

- The loose manhole cover that jiggled metallic for every vehicle that ran over it.

- The beeping gate of the parking garage that rang out like a warning bell.

- The drunken bar hoppers whose fascinating drunk-speak babble was more important than respecting a small micro-budget trying to make its day.

- The rubberneckers who slowed vehicles to gape.

- The vehicles attempting to park in the two parking spaces cleared by the crew to have ample views of the location across the street. Crewmembers were dispatched as living lawn chairs in the great Chicago tradition of saving cleared parking spaces.

- The sirens in the downtown skyscraper chasms howling.

- The skateboarders' click-clacking.

- The Harley engines revving.

- The small dogs being walked whilst yipping-yapping.

- The constant sound of Muddy Waters from a Friday night sports bar.

1.8 Avoid special prop or makeup needs

The goal is to pay for nothing — locations, props, wardrobe. It's unlikely you can get away with that goal for some expenses, but you must consider your options. Your mom runs the local thrift store? Get your props and wardrobe there! Your friend owes you a favor who has a truck that can be shot or used for crew transport? Make the call! Beg and borrow if you can to make your movie!

Thinking of making a vampire or zombie flick? Hope you've got a killer makeup artist because the entire movie depends on his or her handiwork. You wanted horror but didn't have the budget to find a makeup artist (and yes, they cost!) who not only knows about blood effects, but also has the vision to try new looks, something not in the script itself. You're looking for collaborators on all levels and the best people cost more. So, if you'll need special makeup, build that into the budget.

2. B Movies

The granddaddy of the micro-budget, for me, is Roger Corman. By looking at his IMDB page you'll discover he has 410 producer credits and 56 directing credits dating back to 1955. While *Attack of the Crab Monsters* or *Teenage Cave Man* might not make the top 100 movies of all-time, very few men can claim to have a "school" created from their aesthetic. Corman mentored and gave a start to many young film directors such as Ron Howard, Martin Scorsese, and Peter Bogdanovich. He helped launch the careers of actors Peter Fonda and Jack Nicholson. Corman's low-budget B movies made sure the stories reached the largest number of people by telling it in a recognizable genre.

Certain genres always work for a micro-budget such as horror, comedy, thriller, and drama. Corman went one-step further, adding campy comedy to his horror, or thriller aspects to a drama. These were "mash-ups" of genres done with simplicity and for a reasonable price. After you make a hundred of these you would not only know how to bring these in for a price, but for what appeals to a younger audience. Genres to stay away from include period pieces or post-apocalyptic action because the price for these can escalate.

Anyone who's seen Primer knows sci-fi can be done cheap. Robert Rodriguez made *El Mariachi* for the infamous $7,000 so action is also on the list. Look at Fede Alvarez as an example; he wrote and directed the remake of *Evil Dead*. How did a young filmmaker from Uruguay get that gig? He made the short film *Panic Attack!* for $300 and it looked like it was made for $1 million dollars! Based on that short film he got noticed and gained representation in Hollywood. That is how you play the game! Show the Hollywood gatekeepers you can make a high-quality commercial product for dirt cheap.

3. Writing a Logline

A lThe logline is the smallest summation of story. It's a sales tool. It gives a producer or agent or manager a taste of the movie. You want to sell the story, not tell the whole story here.ogline is a brief summary of the film written in 25 words or less. It provides a synopsis of the film's plot as well as an emotional "hook" to stimulate interest.

Loglines terrorize screenwriters, and I understand why. Summing up a 100-page screenplay in one or two sentences isn't easy. The important point is not to overthink it. You only need to remember three things when it comes to loglines:

- Who

- Goal

- Obstacle

You want to *sell* the story, not *tell* the whole story.Here's an example of what we did for *Chat*: "A father searches for his daughter gone missing in the world of cybersex chat." Who is the story about? The father. What is his goal? To find his daughter. What is the obstacle? This shady world of cybersex chat and the nasty fellows he finds there. That's it.

4. Writing the Synopsis

You just wrote a 100-page movie. You want to submit it to a production company, an agency, a management company, or a screenwriting contest, but you need to write a synopsis. No problem, it's only one page. Wait a minute … you need to boil the whole 100 pages into one page? Yep.

If you're trying to find money through the traditional LA sources, the money people are going to want a logline and synopsis. Even if you're going the micro-budget route, you'll need a synopsis for promotional materials, for the Kickstarter fundraising campaign, for potential investors on any level of movie making.

You have to learn how to write a synopsis. In order to do that, you have to come to terms with what your movie is ultimately about.

Understand that a synopsis isn't a treatment. Let's define our terms.

- **Treatment**: Treatments are written in prose paragraph format. You are describing what the camera is seeing now, in real time. The movie plays out for the reader straight from the writer's mind: third-person, present-tense, observable behavior (i.e., nothing in the head such as "he thinks," "she decides," "they consider"). It is written with limited dialogue. It's approximately one page of treatment per 10 pages of the screenplay — on average, up to 30 pages in length.

- **Synopsis**: It's a pitch to sell the story with limited dialogue, secondary characters, subplots, and backstory. You write the elements of the protagonist and antagonist.

Here is an early one-page treatment for *Chat*:

Floating, down a long, narrow corridor in white fluorescent light. Approaching a bathroom door, the door opens wide. White Out. Opening his red-rimmed, bloodshot eyes is Falcon. Knocking a Xanax down with three cups of Espresso, he nervously dresses in a suit and tie, placing on powerful contact lenses and sunglasses. Stranger in a strange land, he enters a nondescript office building. Partial glimpses inside multiple rooms: Chat models in various states of undress, chatting into computer cameras, office cubicles made to look like bedrooms. This is an Adult Chat studio complex, and business is very good.

Falcon stands before Syd, a toad. Syd happens to own this adult chat complex. Falcon has a daughter who has gone missing for a week. Her last contact — working here. Falcon wants answers but Syd, and his Ivy League partner, Geoffrey, offer precious little. Escorting him out, Falcon is told that one of the models, Annie, was a friend of his daughter, Mary Rose.

FLASHBACK. Syd and Annie welcome a new girl to the biz — Mary Rose. Annie will tutor her. Meanwhile Geoffrey pulls Syd aside. He tells Syd he's tired of this business arrangement, that he's carried Syd too long, he is buying him out and has the power to do so. Syd appears at the offices of Doctor Lauren, a Picasso with the liposuction needle. She bankrolled Syd's venture into adult chat. With Syd being cut out, the money train will end for Doctor Lauren, which is unacceptable. She and her partners — some nasty types, including a goon ex-cop named Detective Csonka, demand the money flow continue. She concocts a murder plot.

BACK TO THE PRESENT, Falcon and Annie search for Mary Rose. Clues emerge. Annie discovers a book that was Mary Rose's, and a gun. Falcon breaks into Dr. Lauren's office and is discovered by Csonka, who tortures Falcon with a pair of halogen mag lights. Falcon is knocked out and bloodied. Annie vows to confront Geoffrey the next day and if nothing comes of it, they will go to the police.

FLASHBACK. A woman in a black latex cat suit leads Geoffrey on all fours by his silk Brooks Brothers tie down the fluorescent corridor. They enter the bathroom. Syd and Csonka move with guns from his office, taking positions outside the bathroom door. Syd about to go inside, but stops-looking to Csonka with freaked-out rat's eyes … one more breath … and in he goes.

Opening his red-rimmed, bloodshot eyes is Falcon. Knocking a Xanax down with three cups of Espresso, he nervously dresses in a suit and tie, placing on powerful contact lenses and sunglasses. This is déjavu. The same motions that opened the movie, Falcon with almost identical movements.

Almost.

What follows will be the sound of police sirens, sure, but also the drone of adult webcam chat, echoing from cyberspace and the digital divide. The world will hear about what happened here, and it will become legend, for a news cycle or two, then forgotten. The world will go on, but the revelations will shake Falcon, Mary Rose, and us, to the core.

---

5. Rewriting: Keats Never Did This

I preach "killing the perfectionist" instinct. This means you're going to have to write, and rewrite, and rewrite again. The idea of penning something once that is for the ages might have worked for Percy Shelley or John Keats, but for you, the "unknown" screenwriter, it's not an option.

A great deal depends on the project, and your relationship with those who have creative control. For Jane Doe, I had limited creative control on *any* level. That meant that when my producing team signed the Unapix contract and took their $150,000, we gave up "Final Cut" creative control and became legally responsible to their production demands. That led to difficulties if during the filming of the movie, they're unable to shoot a scene and unable to do pickup afterwards. This means if we don't make our day—meaning get all the filming done scheduled for that day—whatever we don't get is cut from the movie. And if there's no money for pickup days, it means you, as director/ writer, have to make difficult choices if we shoot scene A but run out of time and can't shoot scene B. There is no money in the budget to go back and shoot it later. And tomorrow we're shooting Scene C. Only thing is, Scene C doesn't make sense without Scene B. This is where the writer on set appears and is asked to find a fix.

The writer has to build a bridge from Scene A to Scene C that didn't exist before. There will probably be some dialogue added into Scene C that will accomplish what Scene B was supposed to have done. Figure out what Scene B needed to do and build the bridge.

Same deal when you have to condense an interior scene. The schedule says you've got six pages to shoot but you're running long and won't make it. The director's mind (perhaps you) moves into high-gear plotting on how to make it work. What can be simplified or changed? Can the scene be cut altogether? If you make inter-scene cuts it might lessen the coverage you'll need to shoot it. can be made. Another way to condense the script and save money is by inter-scene dialogue cuts. Example: You have a six page scene you're shooting tomorrow. Examine the scene. Examine places inside the scene where cuts can be made. Make the cuts. This will, almost certainly, save the director time, perhaps lessen the coverage necessary to shoot the scene, and make your production day easier.The script is no longer the prime concern because you've moved beyond script level. You're making the movie now and changes will happen.

There's a famous saying about making a movie: The one you write, the one you shoot, and the one you edit — the final movie. These are usually three very different things. The movie in your mind from months before doesn't much matter when you get into the edit room. What matters is what you got during production, maximizing what you have in the can. For *Chat*, Boris and I had a seven-year-old working relationship going into the project. We signed a contract (see the download kit for details about our screenwriting contract) giving me final say at script level. This was an insurance policy I insisted on after

Jane Doe. Should something happen, nothing would go forward that I didn't feel good about. There was no money into the project yet, the lion's share of work was my own at this point.

Outlining the script for *Chat* took three months. Writing it took another six months. I should say it in the plural: "scripts." I wrote four full drafts before we called it the Shooting Script (White Pages). After that came the sullying of those White Pages with Blue, Green, and Yellow production drafts. After these came on-set "tweaks" — an actor line here, a small interchange for camera purposes there. The script is never done.

5.1 The first five pages of the script

Whether it is a micro-budget or a studio movie, the first five pages of your script is valuable real estate. You've got to nail it or risk losing the reader/audience. All scripts should do four things in the first five pages:

1. Establish the point-of-view character (i.e., protagonist).

2. Establish the tone.

3. Establish the world.

4. Establish the beginnings of conflict.

Let's look at the first draft of Chat, and compare it against what actually became the movie as well as well as some production notes for what happened when we actually filmed it:

Original

```
FADE IN:

INT. CHAT OFFICE HALLWAY — NIGHT (PRESENT DAY)

    Floating, down a fluorescent nightmare. A long,
narrow corridor leads toward a bathroom door. The
door opens wide … WHITE OUT.
```

Final

```
    This scene was shot and edited as is up to the
Rough Cut. The audience feedback we received showed
confusion on this opening so it was swapped out for
a shot of Falcon, our protagonist, in the same chat
office hallway right at the top — less confusing and
more evocative. It also sets up the creepy tone we
want, the lead character, and the world in a single
ten-second shot.
```

Original

    INT. FALCON'S DARK ROOM — DAY

    FALCON, 45, eyes open and ringed red, disturbingly messed up. Dimmer switch at a five-watt flicker. Falcon lays back and listens to a WOMAN'S VOICE.

    WOMAN'S VOICE

    Always the falling, bottomless, silent body, spirit at dawn, dawn on nightmare.

Final

    This was filmed as is, but moved to later on in the film.

Original

    INT. FALCON'S APARTMENT — DAY

    Dim world. Fifteen-watt lightbulbs, pitched blue. Well-kept home of a scientist — doctorate diploma, honors, and awards framed in glass, library of science manuals and biochemistry books — genius stuff.

    RAPID SHOTS — FALCON

    Peeking through blinds, drawing them closed fast. Expertly inserting a set of contacts. The tray with six other pairs of contacts from strong to extreme light protection. Falcon in the medicine cabinet, pops open a large 500-count bottle of Xanax. Knocking the Xanax down with one, two, three cups of espresso. Frail, hair uncut or combed, Falcon nervously dresses in a suit and tie, readying himself.

Final

    This was also filmed as is. It establishes Falcon as a scientist, but also as a man who suffers from photophobia, a disease of the cornea. This is a man who can't handle light, and shuts himself in as a result.

Original

    EXT. FALCON'S APARTMENT — LATER

    Falcon emerges, holding a large wreath, staring up at the sun. He places powerful protective sunglasses over the contacts, stepping into the light.

EXT. STREET — CONTINUOUS

Alien landscape, cars and people move very fast, dizzying. A crying child, a jackhammer at a construction site, the screaming of an EMT van passing with cherry lights blazing. All these exaggerated, hypersensitive for Falcon, who walks with a wreath toward …

EXT. CEMETERY — LATER

Falcon bends, laying the wreath against a newly dug grave. He stands back to observe the wreath, the headstone, the empty cemetery.

EXT. CHAT OFFICE BUILDING — LATER

Falcon looks up at a piece of paper with scrawled writing, then at a nondescript commercial building. He moves inside.

INT. ELEVATOR — CONTINUOUS

Yellow floor numbers pass, reflecting off Falcon's sunglasses, an inexorable rise.

Final

All these scenes were shot as is and open the movie exactly as described. This takes us through about the first two minutes of the movie. Boris felt the pace was good. For me, I felt, and still feel, we could have trimmed time here. Original

INT. CHAT OFFICES — FRONT DESK — CONTINUOUS

A RECEPTIONIST on the phone, Falcon stands before her.

RECEPTIONIST

He's the father. Needs to see her. That's what he says.

INT. SYD'S OFFICE — CONTINUOUS

Falcon timidly, stranger in a strange land, stands before SYD, 48, a toad. As Syd searches the messy office for paperwork. Falcon scans the room …

A video from a liposuction clinic plays on Syd's computer.

Final

Because we shot at Boris' work offices, this scene was moved from Syd's office to the conference room, which gave us more spectacular visuals than a simple office scene. This is a high-profile, upscale establishment, counter to the seedy back room you'd expect of an adult chat-cam operation.

Original

Framed lewd posters advertise the adult webcam operation behind the mahogany desk and office chair.

Looking over paperwork from a file cabinet …

SYD

Like I said, she was only here a week.

Syd hands the application over to the strange, sunglasses-protected Falcon.

SYD

I can see how working a job like this would be concerning for a father.

Maybe their eyes meet; Syd can't penetrate the sunglasses.

Scanning the paperwork …

FALCON

Do you remember her?

SYD

Remember her? Yeah. Bright girl. Liked books, right?

Falcon looks up from the application.

SYD

Didn't leave a forwarding address. They never do.

FALCON

Did she leave anything behind?

SYD

She made some VODs but I don't think you'd want …

A look to Falcon is downright spooky.

SYD

Why would you want those?

FALCON

Maybe I should call the police.

SYD

No … that's all right.

(the toad smiles)

Give me a minute.

Final Script

This stayed in as well because it was a very important establishing scene. Reader/audience has now been introduced to Falcon as a father who is seeking his daughter; she came to work here at this chat operation and was not seen again. Establish Syd as the pockmarked possible villain. Set the movie genre as drama. Set up the beginnings of conflict: Where did his daughter go?

Original

EXT. GEOFFREY'S OFFICE — CONTINUOUS

Syd inside with GEOFFREY, 20s, Ivy-League sharp, handsome. Syd points to Falcon through window blinds. Falcon unable to hear what they're saying, until Syd emerges with Geoffrey.

SYD

This is our studio designer, Geoffrey Davis.

Shaking hands, noting Falcon's agitation …

FALCON

Is there something you remember?

GEOFFREY

I wish there was. In this business girls come and go very quickly. Some don't even finish their first day.

Falcon scans Geoffrey's office … Ivy-League diploma, computer manuals, Silicon Valley literature, and super-powerful computer.

GEOFFREY

I remember your daughter as very intelligent. That's a commodity in short supply around here, right Syd?

SYD

Absolutely.

Final Script

This scene was never shot in Geoffrey's office because it was not needed. We moved Geoffrey into the conference room with the other characters.

Original

INT. CHAT OFFICE HALLWAY — CONTINUOUS

Falcon walks the fluorescent corridor. Still wearing protective sunglasses, he drifts past door after door. Partial glimpses inside … CHAT MODELS in various stages of undress, typing on keyboards or chatting into computer cameras, office cubicles made to look like bedrooms. This is an Adult Chat studio complex and business is very good indeed. Falcon's sunglasses hide his eyes, but the fluorescence still brings pain.

GEOFFREY

We're actually small fish, only 20 studio performers live at this location. One-stop shop, we provide the room, camera, lighting.

Final Script

This scene stayed the same as well. Even though we hint at it, you never explicitly see that we're in a XXX adult cam operation … until here. Our editor and Boris did a great job by "punching" the audience in the face with images from a sleazy world, a backstage look. Boris also did a nice job with the Falcon point of view, to put us right in his head as he walks by room after room of half-dressed women, imagining his own daughter working here.

Original

EXT. ANNIE'S CHAT ROOM — CONTINUOUS

Passing a door, Falcon peeks inside, Geoffrey too.

GEOFFREY

That's Annie. She knew your daughter.

Geoffrey looks back to Syd, who doesn't return the look.

Falcon removes his sunglasses to see a sexy blonde, cutting the air in a pale, pink mini-dress — ANNIE, 27, live online, doing a show. On a wall behind her, a latex-hooded BDSM cat suit, whip, and restraint devices. Annie sees Geoffrey and waves at him. He moves inside to hug her. Syd's sneer relents only when Falcon notices him.

Final Script

This was a short but important scene that made it through to the final. Annie is the co-protagonist of the film and this is the first time Falcon (the main protagonist) sets eyes on her.

Original

INT. FALCON'S APARTMENT — NIGHT

Chat cam installed, computer contrast turned way down, Falcon wears sunglasses as he ties into the chat website. Scanning through webcam listings of women, Falcon stops the browser on the thumbnail of a TATTOOED CAM MODEL, clicking the button for PRIVATE CHAT.

Falcon jumps when, instantly, she appears before him, tattooed along every inch of her body.

Final Script

Stranger in a strange land, Falcon is unaware of such worlds as he plugs into the cybersex world for the first time. We actually shifted this scene down to after he screens the videos of his daughter, and weeps on seeing them.

Thus, we accomplish the four key points in the first five pages of the script — point-of-view of character (Falcon) established; tone (dark) established; world (cyber chat behind the scenes) established; and conflict (a father looking for his daughter in this world that is foreign to him) established.

Making the Movie You Can Afford

When I set out to produce my first feature film, *Fall Away*, I had made a few shorts, and worked for a few years on the budget of *Roundabout American*, the feature I had been wanting to direct. I was approached by an actor I knew who had written the story, had a director attached, and was looking for a producer who could raise the funds and make the shoot happen.

It was 2009 and the world of filmmaking was evolving. Throughout the previous ten years computers and digital cameras had revolutionized the film industry, allowing anyone to make a movie for little to no cost. Digital HD cameras surfaced right and left and the entire postproduction for a feature could now be completed entirely on a laptop with inexpensive software. However, the "standard" dollar amount for an ultra-low budget quality film still ranged between $50,000 and $200,000. Sure, *Paranormal Activity* was about to be released — a major blockbuster that had been made for total budget of $15,000. But *Paranormal Activity* had a total of two actors, one location, and was entirely made of footage captured by a static home video camera that mimicked a surveillance camera.

Fall Away involved ten lead cast members, 12 locations, and a portion of the script had a road movie component that meant taking the entire cast to Nashville for two days in a Winnebago. We were all very clear that we didn't want to compromise quality. The script had a dark, dramatic mood that needed to translate and couldn't be achieved with a camcorder.

I had made short films with good production value on very low budgets, but the lowest was made for $5,000 for a two-day, confined shoot. So when I set out to budget Fall Away, after trimming all the fat and constraining the shoot to 20 days, I still ended up with a $125,000 budget — and that was barebones. It covered locations, minimal crew, gear rental, food, insurance, and cast payments for the union actors.

My main preoccupation was to find funding. Theoretically it should have been easy. The film had a strong gay-centric theme, and the LGBT community is known to support artistic endeavors that spoke about that topic. The lead actor (who had approached me) and myself were contacting everyone we knew to try to get $5,000 to $10,0000 commitments. Despite my long experience fund-raising I was finding this very challenging. We were in the midst of the aftermath of the housing crisis, and the universal response was "Sounds interesting — come back and see me in a year." Everyone we spoke to had lost money on the stock market, and nobody had disposable resources to invest in a film project that had a no-name cast and no distribution secured. Six months went by. We had a total of one commitment for $5,000 and little hope to get the film made by the end of the year.

During that time we had also decided that the director attached to the film might not be the right choice. This is someone who had stage experience, and for whom this would be a first low-budget film. We parted ways with him and went on to find someone with more film experience. We were lucky to find not only what we were looking for, but someone who would bring perspective to our budget concerns.

Julian Grant, who ended up directing the film, had a solid 30 years of experience in the film industry. He had made more than 20 studio feature films, and single-handedly produced and directed the Robocop miniseries that was released in the early 2000s and had been made on a relatively small budget.

After more than 20 years working for studios, Julian decided to move to Chicago from Canada to focus on making smaller, more personal films, where he had full creative control.

When we met him he had just completed his first independent feature, *The Defiled*, a post-apocalyptic zombie film he had made on a four-figure budget. Besides his experience and his creative skills, it was obvious he would be able to make the most of our $125,000 budget, if we could find it.

Unfortunately the summer passed, and by September we still only had $5,000 in commitments, with a potential additional $7,500 on the horizon. Julian had plans for another feature the following summer, and if we didn't shoot over the winter we were likely to lose him. He was getting irritated with my inability to raise the necessary funding, and it was starting to dawn on me that my first experience producing a feature might not happen.

One night in September I was having coffee at Julian's discussing ways to reduce the budget to $100,000 when he interrupted me and asked, "How much do you have right now in commitments?" Taken aback, I told him $12,500 — even though $7,500 of this figure was not completely locked in yet. "OK, then let's make it for $12,500," he said.

I told him that was impossible. Even if it was possible we'd end up with a subpar film, which I wasn't willing to do. I told him that I just couldn't see how to budget a 20-day shoot for $12,500, and that he needed to trust me to find the necessary funding.

The next day he emailed me a $12,500 budget that covered 20 shooting days, telling us he had full confidence in the fact that he could make it happen for that amount and deliver a good-looking, solid film.

Had it been anyone else, I would have laughed it off. However, Julian's credentials were impressive, so was the low-budget science fiction film he had made the previous summer, and he definitely looked like someone who knew what he was talking about. So I read through his budget and started thinking about how to make it happen.

He kept everything in the script, redistributed roles, cut pay to zero for the entire crew including himself, cut the location budget to a few hundred dollars, and zeroed out everything that was not strictly impossible to get for free. He would shoot and edit the film himself, eliminating the need for a director of photography and an editor. He would adapt his vision to the locations we could find for free or cheap, and work with a nonunion cast.

I would actively produce on set and handle the day-to-day budget, eliminating the need for a line producer or production manager.

I would also organize casting, eliminating the need for a casting director. We were lucky enough to have found another coproducer who was a senior sound designer and composer, so she would take care of everything sound related. Our crew of 40 became a crew of 7. The catered food became homemade chili. The Nashville trip would be accomplished by shooting inside the Winnebago on the way down, then spending two nights at a Red Roof Inn with a skeleton crew with three people per room. Most importantly, we would shoot on weekends only, eliminating the need for cast and crew members to give up other professional activities or income during the shoot, and allowing them to accept zero up-front salary.

We made the film over eight weekends, mostly in January of 2010, with a couple of additional weekends in April (notably the trip to Nashville).

The final budget ended up closer to $20,000 than $12,500. We could have made it for the original budget, but something interesting happened. Once I went back to my contacts saying "We're making this film in January," some people who had turned me down previously all of the sudden agreed to invest small amounts. We had gone from a project that couldn't get its funding to a project that was funded and happening. We were looking for solutions to the problems the budget was creating for us instead of trying to tailor the budget to the problems that might happen. I was focused on making a film instead of stressing out about finding money.

Of course, we had a few advantages that helped such as we had an experienced director who also knew how to shoot his own film and edit it. We also overcame challenges that previously seemed unrealistic to me with so little money. I managed very large budgets in past entrepreneurial experiences — here I was denying $10 requests from Julian for an additional lens he wanted to rent. I learned that preconceived ideas about budgets were not valid, and that within the boundaries of reason, films could be made for a fraction of the cost they were first thought to require. Most importantly, I learned that letting the budget get in the way of making a film is a certain path to not making the film, and that if you're serious about independent film, you need to make your film work within the parameters of the funding you have, or make another film that fits.

1. Scheduling

Before we dive into the specifics of constructing a budget, let's talk about scheduling. Even though the actual schedule is built by the first assistant director closer to the shoot, any line producer who attempts to put together a rational budget needs to first construct a reasonable rough shooting schedule that best reflects what is achievable based on the current draft of the script.

Every element in a budget is based on the number of shooting days. Cast and crewmembers are paid either daily or weekly, so you need to know (or rather estimate at this stage) how many days each will be required for. Locations will also charge by the day, so you have to guess how many days you'll be spending in each location. Same for all rentals, food, and everything that is not a one-time purchase.

As most people know, films are generally shot out of script order, for practical reasons but also for financial reasons. It is usually less expensive to rent equipment, employ cast, and use locations on consecutive shooting days than it is when the schedule is broken up. Notwithstanding the practicalities of having to move in and out of locations (and possibly redress them every time), rates for rentals tend to be lower when you can group things.

The problem is that when you craft an initial budget with the goal of raising funds, most constraints tend to be unknown. You don't know what cast will be available. You don't know what your locations will be or when you'll be allowed to shoot there so you estimate the best you can, giving yourself enough buffer space to be flexible when reality kicks in.

The first step is to break down the script scene by scene, log the page count for each scene, and group them by location first, then by cast. For example, if you have ten scenes that take place in a given location, and five cast members over the ten scenes, put the ten scenes together and then group them so the same cast members are closest together. The reasoning is that cast members are paid daily, so the fewer days you can condense a given cast member's presence on set, the less expensive it will be.

Once your script is broken down and ordered in that fashion, place scenes in days based on page counts. General rule of thumb is that you can shoot five pages per working day. On independent shoots that rate tends to often be closer to seven, eight, or sometimes up to ten pages a day. But for the purposes of a preliminary budget, I would stick to five pages per day. This way you maintain the required flexibility to adjust once things take shape. If I have a heavy dialogue scene that I know the director will likely want to shoot on a tripod with little camera movement and that accounts for six pages, followed by a four-page action/fight scene that will require blocking on set, numerous takes, and art resets, I will feel comfortable giving one day to each scene even though one is a 50 percent heavier page count than the other. It's a much smarter choice than breaking up the first scene (something that should usually be avoided at all costs if possible) and trying to fit five pages in each day.

Once you have roughly arranged your scenes by day and location, you will have a first glimpse at the number of shooting days required to complete the picture. Hopefully it should be close to your total number of script pages divided by five. If it's much higher than that, go back and see how you can rearrange and regroup things to merge a couple of days together. By carefully analyzing the factors that are taking your schedule over the hoped for amount of days you can usually come up with solutions, or identify scenes that could be problematic.

The last step in completing a preliminary schedule is to take into account some basic expected location constraints. If you're shooting in a restaurant, you can assume that you will need to shoot at night or in the morning (assuming you don't have the budget to shut down the restaurant). Try to group your day scenes with your day scenes as much as possible, and your night scenes with your night scenes, to minimize the burden on the cast and crew (scheduled shifts are difficult on everyone). If you run into issues, see what scenes could be shot day for night or night for day.

The idea is not to spend days on this or to get into too much detail, as things will shift once you actually hire cast and find locations, but to make some reasonable assumptions that will allow you to map the costs in an intelligent manner so you don't get hit by one bad surprise after the another when things become real.

2. Learning to Adapt

Because you can now make movies for a fraction of what they used to cost doesn't mean you can make anything for any budget. The ability to make a film for a given budget involves certain constraints, and often requires flexibility and agility to make it happen. Even armed with those skills, the script needs to lend itself to it.

Based on my experience with *Fall Away*, I revisited *Roundabout American*, the film I previously tried to get made. *Roundabout American* was a very different film, a broad comedy that was supposed to showcase America seen through the eyes of a young French guy, a fish-out-of-water story that needed to showcase the grandeur and decadence of modern America.

A couple years prior, when I had completed a first draft of the script, I had paid $1,500 out of my pocket to hire a line producer to create a budget for it. She had worked for two weeks straight and had landed with a roughly $1 million budget, which she had presented to me as "bare bones." It did involve some decent amounts for the lead actors, and would nicely cover the 60 or so cast members and the 45 locations that included a penthouse filled with marble bathtubs for the climax of the film — and the opening scene that took place in the immigration arrival hall at Chicago O'Hare's airport — nothing less.

Since then I had worked on raising that money. I had actually been more successful than with *Fall Away*, mostly due to two reasons. First, I had been raising these funds before the housing collapse, and second, the film had a much broader mass appeal. I had managed to collect $140,000 in written, signed commitments. The problem was that this still only represented 15 percent of my budget, and that these commitments were set to expire in 2010 if I was unable to move forward with the film.

On the 16th day of shooting *Fall Away*, while Julian was directing a closed set scene that involved nudity — which meant I wasn't allowed on the actual set and had to lock myself in a room for four hours without the privilege of peeking, I decided I was going to use the lessons I had learned, and would make *Roundabout American* for $140,000. I started fresh on a brand new, scaled-down budget that would allow me to shoot the film with the funds I theoretically had. I applied all the lessons I had learned from Julian meticulously. Of course, the parameters were different. With 40 locations we couldn't constrain ourselves to shooting a single location in a day to avoid the expense of a unit move. We couldn't count on the fact that all cast members will behave like a big family and will tolerate eating home-cooked food every day. I also didn't have the ability like Julian to shoot and light my own film. I needed a director of photography and equipment, and even my longtime collaborator Fred Miller would need support to fill that role.

I went line by line, trimming every bit of fat I could find. After a few hours I happily rested my pen — I had gone from a budget of $1 million to the budget of $200,000! Still $50,000 more than what I had, but so much closer. Armed with my *Fall Away* experience, where more money had started coming in once I had announced the film was moving forward, and with my eye on the stock market which was starting climb back up, I figured I could find the remaining $50,000 and get it done.

Because I was directing this one (my first feature in that role), and didn't have the bandwidth to fill both roles of producer and director, I needed to find a producer. Who could be better than the person who had taught me to craft such a budget and who I had just worked with on another film? Julian.

The problem was that Julian wasn't interested in producing other people's projects. He had moved to Chicago to make his own. He had chosen creative freedom over the income he could claim producing and directing larger films. The only reason for him to produce someone else's film was if that gave him enough money to justify not making one of his own during that time. Also note that when I reduced the budget from $1 million to $200,000 the producer's salary went down from $50,000 to a meager $5,000.

When I queried Julian while we were driving to Nashville for the last weekend of shooting *Fall Away*, he politely turned me down. So I insisted, and asked him to at least read the script. A couple months went by — I had lost hope at that point and was trying to find someone else — when I got an email from Julian on the fourth of July.

"I'm 80 pages in and want to make it if we have enough money. It's too big for $200k even with all of our tricks. Will advise. Happy July 4. JG"

My first reaction was "What?" Julian, who had reduced the *Fall Away* budget from $125,000 to 10 percent of that figure, who had taught me everything I knew about budgeting, who had hammered in me the motto: "Make the movie with what you have," was now telling me we couldn't make this film because $200,000 wasn't enough?

Once we met I understood what he was trying to say. His concern was that my vision would not be fully realized. He knew this was a passion project — the first script I had written, and my first feature as a director — and felt that some of the compromises that needed to be made to deliver this film for $200,000 might be hard for me to come to terms with. At the end of the day he was ready and able to get it made for the $140,000 I had in the bank, but the film would suffer.

We listed the areas where it would suffer, and what was acceptable to me and what wasn't. We wanted to make sure that if we embarked on that road we could make a film that we would be proud of making.

The high-rise penthouse with the marble bathtubs was the first to go. It became a ground floor mansion a friend of ours was willing to rent at a reasonable cost. I was OK with that. The immigration hall at O'Hare airport became the departure area at the Rockford regional airport, redressed to look like immigration. The crane shots I had envisioned for some scenes in the film became low-angle shots that achieved a different effect but worked just as well.

Step by step I had to adapt my vision. Sometimes it was easy, sometimes it was not. Sometimes I'd get angry and plainly say no, to which Julian would respond, "No problem. We keep the crane shot. Just let me know which scene you'd like to cut to pay for it." But then I'd think that's how he probably felt when I was denying him his $10 lens rentals on Fall Away, and I learned to slowly adapt to reality and make choices that were realistic within the budget we had, and would not heavily compromise the integrity of what I was trying to portray.

The final budget for *Roundabout American* came in at $195,000, and looking back I can honestly say that any flaws the film came from directorial choices I made — not from lack of money.

3. Budgeting Levels

When the time came to make *Chat* (my third film), the scenario was again different. Paul and I had set out from the start to craft a movie that could be made for as low as $25,000. In other words, using little cast and few, fairly nondescript locations.

After Paul turned in his first draft of the script I started the budgeting. Not knowing this time how much we'd be able to raise, I prepped four different budgets, ranging from $25,000 to $100,000 in $25,000 increments. Being both the director and lead producer on this film, I was determined to give myself flexibility, and to sacrifice as little of the vision I had for the film as possible in each scenario. I felt confident that I could make an almost equally good film for $25,000 as for $100,000. The big difference was comfort.

What exactly does "comfort" mean? Here is an excerpt from the email I sent to Paul when I forwarded the budgets to him:

- $100,000 is ideal ($130,000 with tax credit), including all the bells and whistles.

- $75,000 is the minimum to be able to qualify for the tax credit ($100,000 spend, $25,000 back = $75,000). We cut some salaries, then spend on camera and locations, you and I don't get paid at all, and we can't pick SAG actors for every part, but for the majority. We're in decent shape.

- $50,000 is the big jump (really cut in half from the $75,000 since there's no tax credit anymore). Department heads get paid symbolically a few hundred dollars each, others don't at all, and we can only cast three SAG actors (budgeted for the three leads), and some leads would have to be non-SAG and most day players unpaid. We shoot on whatever camera we can get for free, and trim all the fat where we can. Art and locations money is significantly reduced. We'll have to work with the locations we can find at our price point and not dress them much (all money should go to dress the girls' rooms).

- $25,000 means no one gets paid, no SAG actors at all (or one SAG actor and everyone else unpaid). Barebones as it can get. Really not ideal, but feasible. With that said the major difference is we don't pay people at all. Will the lost $100,000 discourage our longtime collaborators from working? Probably not.

- If we can get close to $50,000, we should strive to hit $75,000 as we can then claim the tax credit and are really up to $100,000. But if all we can muster is $25,000, we can still do it.

We'll come back to tax credit questions in Chapter 6, but a few things jump out here. The biggest difference between the sample budget levels were salaries. What salaries translate to is the quality of people with whom you work — quality of the cast and lead crew. In our case, we were lucky. Paul had been active in the Chicago theater scene for more than 15 years, which meant he had access to brilliant stage actors who might not be in SAG if it came down to us being unable to afford union rates. I had enough contacts through my previous experiences to ensure that I could pull in a few talented and experienced people to head most departments, who might accept to work unpaid or at a very low rate because of our past work together. We also had a script that seemed to pique interest.

The reason I was comfortable making this film for $25,000 was because I had figured out through my previous experiences how to best utilize the funding if we were to have to do this at the lowest possible budget level. The following sections are a few key rules I learned the hard way for a super-tight budget.

3.1 Get the best cast you can

A film is a script and cast. My DP and my composer will hate me when they read that, but everything else is frosting on the cake! I would sacrifice everything else to be able to afford the actors I think are best for the lead roles. I've worked with nonunion actors who were stellar, but being able to afford SAG actors means *choice* — and choice is key.

This portion of the budget is not so much about the fact that a more expensive cast is better; it's about being able to afford a more expensive cast if they are the best fit for your parts. On several shorts I shortchanged cast due to budget, so I could allocate money towards other departments: *This is the biggest mistake any filmmaker can make.* When you create the budget, start with the cast, and assume that as many of your leads as your budget will allow are SAG. You can always reallocate the funds to other departments if you find perfect matches who agree to work unpaid.

3.2 Save money for postproduction

Postproduction, as cheap as it can be budgeted, is rarely free. Even if you know how to edit a film yourself, you will likely need some form of postproduction sound, score, and quite likely some basic visual effects to correct mistakes made on the shoot. One of the biggest mistakes junior filmmakers make is to allocate all available money to production, with the idea that "we'll worry about postproduction later." The problem with that reasoning is that once you're done with shooting, you will want to have the security of knowing that you can actually complete the film in a timely manner; otherwise, all the effort put in so far was for nothing.

I was recently talking with a first-time filmmaker who told me his film had been in postproduction for eight years, all because he was short the $20,000 he needed for postproduction. He had spent more than $150,000 on shooting the film, but couldn't find enough to hire an editor and a sound designer to complete it. Imagine that nightmare! Stuck waiting eight years to complete the film. So, when you budget your film, set aside some funding for postproduction and keep it in a separate bank account so the temptation to spend it during the shoot doesn't become overwhelming.

3.3 Save money for festivals

The golden rule preached by every film production book is the 50 percent rule. Take your budget, split it in half, and spend half on getting the film made, and half on marketing and distribution. For many reasons this is neither practical nor really necessary nowadays for most independent filmmakers, but do set aside some cash to be able to submit to festivals once your film is complete.

A full one-year festival submission cycle if you do all the majors and a few minors is about $3,000 to $4,000. Set this amount aside so you can get eyes on your film as soon as possible once it is complete.

3.4 Keep a contingency fund

The excuses not to plan for a contingency fund are plenty — and they're all bad. A standard motion picture contingency is 10 percent of the entire budget. Realistically, most indie films can't allocate this much, but shoot for 5 percent at the very least. If you don't plan for a decent contingency, and additional unavoidable expenses surface, guess what's going to become your contingency funding? The postproduction and festival money. This will lead you to the scenarios described in the previous points — with no money to complete the film or to get it seen at festivals.

One very important thing to note: Budgeted contingency is not meant to fill in for other risk factors that are traditionally budgeted such as overtime for cast, equipment loss and damage, or insurance deductibles. These are items that you need to expect to pay and that have their own line items in the budget. The contingency is for the unexpected; the things that you forgot to account for or that happen and could not be predicted such as the crewmember who parked in a tow zone and wants his tickets reimbursed, or the location that tells you the day before you're shooting that it has decided to increase its rental fee.

4. Budgeting: Four Categories

Film budgets usually break down in four main categories — above the line, below the line, postproduction, and other costs.

4.1 Above the line

The term "above the line" is used to represent the creative talent costs and usually includes items associated with the cast, director, producer, and writers of a film. On a major motion picture above-the-line costs can sometimes make up 50 percent or more of the budget of a film. On micro-budget films they usually represent anywhere between 10 and 20 percent of the budget, as most of the funding goes towards below-the-line costs and indispensable elements that actually get the film made.

4.1a Development

Development costs usually include any expenses incurred during the very early stages of conceptualizing a film, including research, budget preparation for fundraising, expenses tied to fund-raising, etc. I won't cover those in detail here as on a DIY film these usually don't exist or have been paid out-of-pocket by the filmmakers long before the funding for the film was raised.

4.1b Story and other rights

This includes any costs associated with creating the script. This usually includes writer fees and payment of rights if the script was acquired or is an adaptation of an existing work. Again, this is usually minimal on DIY films, although you may have to pay a writer contingent on fund-raising if you decide to hire a professional writer to work on your script (a wise decision if you ask me, unless you are yourself are a competent writer with experience).

4.1c Producer's unit

Costs associated with the producers of the film and any crew that work directly with them throughout the entire life of the project (meaning excluding production managers or production coordinators whose role is usually confined to the shooting period). This usually means the line producer and any coproducers.

The lead producer's salary is generally 5 percent of the entire budget, but on smaller films it often ends up being deferred or reduced to nothing. Depending on the relationship you have with your producer, and how involved he or she is in the project, you may be able to avoid this cost entirely. However it is worth spending a small portion of your budget getting an experienced producer on board who can facilitate and organize things as needed. On smaller features the producer often ends up filling in as the line producer as well since there is usually no budget to pay both.

4.1d Director's unit

This category includes all costs associated with the director of the film. Realistically speaking, on a DIY film, the director's salary is the last thing to be paid, and will often end up serving as a contingency, unless the creator of the project is a producer and/or writer and a director has been hired.

If you're reading this book and are planning to make a film, chances are you are the director, and if so, you will likely end up forfeiting the 5 percent of the budget that is usually attributed to this position. As much as it would be nice to get paid making a film, if it is your project, you will usually want to put that salary towards elements that can make the film better.

On *Roundabout American*, my $10,000 salary ended up going towards a large mansion for a pivotal scene in the film and a better camera. On Chat, the budget was low enough that I forfeited my salary, knowing that the $2,500 was much better spent on elements that could actually serve the film.

4.1e Talent

The decision of how to allocate funding towards cast is one of the most crucial and difficult to make. Depending on the budget of your film, and the goals you have for the picture once it is completed, these costs can vary dramatically.

As mentioned earlier, you want to try to preserve the flexibility to hire union (SAG) talent for your film, if possible. Let's start with a breakdown of the standard rates for union talent.

- For budgets $200,000 and less, you will find yourself signing an Ultra-Low Budget Agreement with SAG and paying any union cast $125 per eight-hour day of shooting. [1]

- For budgets between $200,000 and $625,000, you are under the Modified Low-Budget Agreement and paying your cast a day rate of $335 or a weekly rate of $2,190 (hence the benefit of grouping your cast as much as possible since the weekly rate offers a discount over the day rate).

- For budgets $625,000 to $2.5 million, your day rate climbs to $630 and your weekly rate to $2,190.

---

1 "Low-Budget Film Actors to Get 25-Percent Pay Hike Under New SAG-AFTRA Contracts," David Robb, *Deadline Hollywood*, accessed March 2015. http://deadline.com/2015/01/sag-aftra-low-budget-actors-contract-pay-hike-1201347137/

I'll stop here as anything above this is outside the scope of this book and falls under the SAG basic agreement with significantly higher rates.

For all of the above, overtime (i.e., hours past the first eight hours in a day) is then prorated at a higher rate in such a manner that if you keep an actor on set for 12 hours you will pay almost double the day rate. This means that you have a strong incentive to try to keep individual cast member days within the initial eight hours, if possible (which is often challenging on micro-budget films).

Of these, only the Ultra-Low Budget Agreement allows for the employment of both union and nonunion cast. Anything that is in the $200,000 and more range forces you to pay all your talent union rates (and nonunion members will be funneled into the path to join the union on their next union shoot).

All the rates listed above are also minimal rates. What this means is that any actor can negotiate a higher rate with the production at will. In other words, if you are trying to bring name talent to your project, don't expect the person to be willing to work for the rates listed above, he or she will likely request a higher salary to join the project.

With all this established, the following are a few thoughts to consider when budgeting your talent costs.

There is a strong incentive to try to stick to the lower budget levels. If the initial budget comes in at $250,000, try to work hard to bring down to $200,000 or less. The fact of climbing to the next SAG-budget level increases your budget by doubling your cast levels at every level (and by the same token, if your budget is $250,000 and $50,000 of it is talent, you will automatically save $30,000 by dropping to less than $200,000, meaning you only have to save an additional $20,000 to get to the desired level).

Name actors or no-name actors? That's a difficult debate, and often a hard choice to make. The general answer (and we'll come back to this in Chapter 9 — marketing and distribution) is that your film will become infinitely more sellable if you can get name talent, and that you should make every effort to bring some in even if it means trimming production expenses.

Unless you have connections to name talent that allow you to convince them to work on the project at union rates, it's generally unrealistic to think of bringing in anyone remotely famous for less than

$2,500 daily. If your budget is less than $100,000 you may have a hard time getting a name attached. You may be better off investing the 10 or 20 percent of the budget this single person would cost into your film. If your budget is larger, you definitely want to allocate some money towards name talent.

If you can get your budget to the SAG Ultra Low-Budget Agreement level, try a mix of union and nonunion talent. Nonunion talent will usually work for free as they are actors who are either starting out and want to build a portfolio, or actors who don't usually do much film (stage actors) and may be interested in making a movie for the experience. On both *Roundabout American* and *Chat*, we budgeted union talent for the lead parts where we wanted to preserve the flexibility of hiring from a larger pool, nonunion for the secondary parts and day players.

Always budget for overtime. Remember that on a micro-budget or low-budget feature your days will usually be closer to 12 hours than 8 (this is actually true even on very large budget films, as the cost savings associated to shooting fewer, longer days usually outweigh by far the costs associated to scheduling and paying for additional days of shooting). Depending on how your schedule comes together, it is safe to plan for half the cast days to be 12-hour days. Having that overtime covered gives you an allowance that you can then redistribute at will.

No need to try to break down the overtime by cast members at the early budgeting stage, just add up your total man days for your entire cast and allocate 75 percent of the base rate applied to those days for overtime. For example, if you are on a SAG Ultra-Low Budget Agreement, and your union cast is expected to spend 100 days of shooting (five cast members at 20 days each), allow for 50 days at $75 or $3,250 for overtime.

Finally, don't forget to budget for the SAG pension and health costs for your union talent. Those will vary over time but were around 19 percent as of this writing.

Even if the story you're writing is character-driven, it doesn't mean you'll need ten principle and secondary characters to tell it. I would suggest limiting key characters to five or less. Think about it, $125 per actor per day? Your team cannot afford to spend that on ten actors and maintain a budget. Another important note is that you most definitely don't want to get into the habit of paying some of your actors and not others. Even the non-SAG actors should get a nominal fee. Force yourself to make sure every character has a purpose. Limit the number of extras and crowd scenes.

4.2 Below the line

Below the line represents all direct production costs; meaning anything that takes place during the preproduction and shooting period of a film.

4.2a Production staff

The production staff includes everyone associated with handling the day-to-day aspects of the production and the shoot and who are not technicians (i.e., people with specific technical skills). Most important on the list are the production manager and his or her production coordinator, and the first and second assistant directors.

The production manager and coordinator are the immediate arms of the producer and line producer during the preproduction and the production team. They handle all day-to-day operations, coordinate all logistical aspects of the shoot, and make sure that whatever needs to be there on a given shooting day is there on time and under budget (hopefully). The reality of micro-budget does mean that with a budget of $50,000 or less you can't afford to spend money on these roles, and even with $100,000, you may want to spend a minimal amount here, and allocate funds to technical roles that require pointed skills such as an outstanding director of photography, better sound, etc.

The good news is that because this is a nontechnical skill that requires some previous film experience, but can be learned with the help of a solid producer and good common sense, you usually have the option to hire someone who may still be in film school or wants the credit and will often agree to work for no pay. If your producer is solid and the unit production manager (UPM) and production coordinator are intelligent and motivated, they will quickly learn the ropes.

On *Fall Away*, because our budget was so minimal, I was cutting down on free crew to save money on food. I worked with a single production manager and no production coordinator. That production manager was an aspiring filmmaker, who had minimal set experience, but managed to efficiently handle all aspects of the production with some guidance. On *Chat*, our production manager was a film student who had never filled that position before but excelled at it because he was motivated and quick to learn.

As mentioned in Chapter 2, the first assistant directors (ADs) are so critical to the shooting process and the success of the film that I would strongly advise finding some money if needed to compensate someone who has filled that position in the past, preferably multiple times. It takes a very specific personality to be a good AD, and good ADs don't come along often, let alone for free. So when budgeting, if you have X dollars left over after budgeting all the absolutely essential paid posts, consider weighing these dollars towards hiring a competent first assistant director. It's a decision that may save you money and time every single day of the shoot and pay for itself.

4.2b Production design and art direction (set construction, set decoration, props)

Production design and art direction, along with all the various subdepartments that fall under those, can vary drastically from film to film, and can be one of the trickiest departments to budget properly. As with everything, getting the right person to do the job is absolutely critical. You need your production designer to be not only a gifted artist, but someone who has a very strong ability to create and maintain a decent budget for his or her department. As opposed to most other areas where the expenses are generally spread somewhat evenly over the span of a shoot, the production design budget will fluctuate drastically from day to day and from location to location.

Before writing in a final figure for art into your budget, you need your production designer to turn over a detailed, location-by-location breakdown of what he or she plans on doing, what materials and crew he or she will need on each day, and how far ahead he or she needs the funds released to him or her for a given location.

In the films I have made, I worked with several talented production designers who ended up being a disaster as the shoot unfolded. The most common situation being beautiful mockups being shown during preproduction for all locations, but poor estimation of costs. The end result was that the first location looked great, the second one not so good, and on the third I'd get hit with a request for more funding that was not available.

Therefore, when vetting a production designer, make sure that in addition to the creative skills, he or she also knows how to plan and budget adequately, and release the funding to the person in increments.

When budgeting on production design for a micro-budget film, you will usually need to strongly arbitrate what is most important to you. When you're shooting a film for $50,000 or $100,000 there isn't enough money to grant the director his or her wishes in every location. Start thinking about which sets will most benefit from production design money. When visiting locations, take into consideration how close they are to your vision of the film. One of the keys to saving on production design is by spending the extra time to scout locations until you have found one that matches your vision closely enough so you don't have to dress it much. Sometimes it may even make sense to spend additional money on a specific location so you can save more on dressing it.

As far as how much of the budget should be allocated to art, that's a question to which the answer greatly varies from film to film, depending on the genre, the time period, and the number of locations. If you're doing a period piece, it will end up being a substantial portion of the budget. If you're making a contemporary drama in nondescript locations, it may end up being a very small portion. On *Fall Away*, our production design budget was a grand total of $300.

Even if you feel there is no production design involved, make sure to hire at least one person for the job. Production design is not just the art of creating sets, it's also augmenting the existing, and complements the photography and other visual elements of the film even in scenarios where there is nothing obvious to be done. A candle or a poster placed judiciously in your frame can make a shot go from bland to interesting, and if you don't have a dedicated person to think this over, you will end up losing time on set by having other people fill in.

4.2c Director of photography, cameras, and lenses

The evolution of cameras and technology over the past ten years has made shooting high-quality, high-definition digital films at a marginal cost a reality for thousands of independent filmmakers around the world. How to budget for the visuals of your film depends on what your goals are and the nature of the project. With the right person at your side, you accomplish a lot for very little.

I've been fortunate enough to have found a director of photography (DP) who I not only work well with, but who also fully understands the budgetary constraints on an independent film and is capable of adapting and making a lot happen with very little.

I've worked with Fred Miller on seven films now, and I am always impressed with what he can do with a camera and floor lamp. Finding the right person who understands your style, can work quickly, and with very little, can save you a lot of money in other areas. In my opinion, it's well worth allocating a salary to that position even on the smallest budgets. Sure, you'll find tons of students or recent graduates who will be willing to work for free in order to get a DP credit. Some may even be very talented. However, they will likely not have the experience necessary to consistently deliver beautiful footage in a timely manner, or to work with a limited crew when needed. The bottom line, it is preferable to allocate most or all the salary in the camera department to a good DP, rather than spread it across many crewmembers and get a less experienced department head.

The biggest visual cost is the rental or acquisition of a camera. There are cameras that will produce an excellent image quality for a total acquisition cost of $1,500 or less. The advent of the Canon DSLRs, notably the 7D and 5D models, have made high definition, film like video production available to anyone. Should you want to shoot in 4K resolution, you can go with a RED or a Blackmagic, but the cost will be higher.

In my opinion, if your budget is limited, you are better off going with a less expensive, 1080P camera, than spending the money to shoot 4K. The reason is that most indie films are released on DVD and VOD, where the 4K footage will be reconverted to 1080P anyway. 4K is the way of the future, but not widespread enough to be a requirement for indie filmmaking. A good DP who knows how to use a camera will produce beautiful imagery on a lower resolution camera. When I first met Fred Miller in the early 2000s, he had just finished shooting a film on a Panasonic DVX 100, one of the first 24P cameras that wasn't even shooting basic HD (imagine that). I watched a clip recently, and despite the resolution being about 16 times lower than 1080P, the film is gorgeous.

If your budget is so small that it doesn't allow you to rent or purchase the camera you really want, one trick I've used many times is to buy it and then resell it later. You basically buy a brand new (or slightly used) camera at the beginning of the shoot using your postproduction budget to acquire it, and then resell it immediately after principal photography is done. You can expect to lose 10 percent or so of the value if you negotiate the purchase and sale well enough; or sometimes you can even make a few dollars if you buy a used camera at a really great price on Craigslist and resell it a few weeks later!

Another consideration depending on the nature of your shoot is whether to budget for one or two cameras. Using the buy and resell strategy, getting a second camera may not add up to much, and may save you hours if not days of shooting, with everything it entails. If your film is dialogue heavy in particular, having two cameras will allow you to shoot your mediums and close-ups in one take instead of two, effectively halving the shooting time for some scenes. Discuss it with your DP, but this is a technique that even on lower budget films can save a lot of money in the overall budget for a small additional one-time cost.

The last element to take into account when budgeting for camera equipment is the lenses. Every DP will tell you that the quality of your lenses will deeply affect the quality of the image. I would, without a doubt, shoot a film on a slightly lower quality camera if it allowed me to rent higher quality lenses. Lenses are usually relatively inexpensive on a daily basis, but can add up over time. One great resource is the advent of online rental sites for lenses such as BorrowLenses.com, which will ship you a lens for a rental as short as one day at a fraction of the cost your local rental house will charge.

4.2d Camera crew

Depending on your director of photography's requests, your camera crew may be as small as a single-assistant camera, or as large as ten people. I generally try to avoid large camera crews on micro-budget shoots, mostly for space reasons. You often find yourself crammed into ridiculously small locations where each body reduces the usable space.

The camera crew can usually be made up of solid students who will work for low- or nonexistent-day rates, and for these positions it is very feasible to have a rotation depending on the day so the time is split to accommodate unpaid crewmembers' availability. It's also an area where it is easy to entice people to work for free or cheap by giving them an additional credit that will propel them further in their career. Let your first-assistant camera shoot some B-Roll with the second camera, and all of a sudden he or she is now a second unit director of photography. The Second AC fills in for him or her with the DP during that time, and he or she is now an additional First AC.

4.2e Gaffers, grips, and lights

A good gaffer is essential, and if you have room for another paid position in the camera, grip, and electrical departments on top of your director of photography (DP), that's where the money should go. A bad gaffer can slow down the shoot, and more importantly be a hazard to your crew. A good gaffer can make the DP's job considerably easier.

I've worked on shoots with Fred where we had incompetent or unmotivated gaffers, and I cringed every time I saw Fred having to leave the camera to go adjust a light himself. A lot of gaffers also own light packages, and you may be able to save quite a bit of money by hiring a gaffer along with his or her lighting package, rather than having to rent from a rental house. Usually a gaffer who works on a set will rent his or her lights for less than or half the cost of renting the equivalent from a big rental house. The rest of the grip and electrical crew is usually unpaid on low-budget shoots, and that's another area where it is fairly easy to organize a rotation of various people depending on availabilities.

4.2f Production sound

The biggest mistake new filmmakers make is not allocating enough budget to production sound. It may shock you to find out that production sound can cost as much for a two-person crew as the entire camera crew including the director of photography (DP) and their gear. Good production sound people are scarce, and they don't work for cheap. It is a highly technical skill, that is not very recognized creatively, so people who are good at it have no incentive to work for free or cheap. If your film gets into a lot of festivals and/or gets distribution, your DP will possibly come out with praise in the press, some awards, and a huge boost in his or her career. Your location sound mixer not so much.

A qualified sound mixer will usually not work for less than $300 per day of shooting. Multiply that by 20 days (yes, sound is something you need every day) and about 11 percent of your $50,000 budget is gone. Meanwhile your DP is making a meager $100 per day. And guess what? It's worth it. A bad location sound mixer can mean spending this daily rate for every *hour* of studio time to rerecord and loop scenes that are otherwise unusable. Not to mention the performance deterioration of an actor who is looping a scene in a studio.

On one of my films I had hired a two-person sound crew for a discounted rate. The deal was that the main sound mixer, who had come recommended, had committed to another project on Saturdays and that his boom operator would be mixing on those days instead of him. On the first Saturday of the shoot, we were shooting a scene in a

150-square-foot basement. I called roll, and simultaneously the furnace turned on emitting a loud whistling noise. I waited for our boom op/sound mixer to ask me to cut, but he didn't react. Finally I called cut and ask him how bad the issue was. He gave me a blank stare, looked at his mixer, and uttered "I don't think it's an issue, my meter's not picking it up." Fred and I looked at each other and knew we had a problem. Six months later, when I got to the studio for post sound, I was told that most of what we had recorded on Saturdays was unusable.

Location sound issues can be extremely costly to try to fix in post-production, and may involve bringing in actors for multiple additional days to Automated Dialogue Replacement (ADR) entire scenes, so the money you saved by hiring a junior sound engineer for cheap will end up spent later.

Also, do not discount the importance of good sound for distribution. It's actually one of the elements a distributor will take into consideration first. Films with bad or noisy audio are the first to be eliminated. Studies have shown that an audience will prefer the same film with a washed out, lower quality image, and good sound, than the same with perfect picture and a noisy, uneven mix.

4.2g Effects (mechanical and special)

For low-budget movies the most common use of onset effects is for gunfire, which can be a fairly hefty cost. If you are planning to have onset guns and/or gunfire, try to cram it all in one day of shooting if possible, and budget a solid $2,000 per day. In order to have a non-plastic gun on set, you need to pay a certified weapon wrangler, a member of the police force at union rates to watch over the set, and the cost of squibs, ammo, gun rentals, etc.

4.2h Set operations

Set operations covers all the miscellaneous costs of running a set, the largest of which is generally food and/or craft service. Within the boundaries of reason try not to skimp too much on these. Generally you can account for an average of $7 to $8 per main meal, and $5 per second meal per person. It's often tempting to try to save a few dollars by getting the less expensive sodas and snacks, but it's usually a mistake.

I had a set where the producer had gotten the local, cheapest brand of cola, and probably saved $5 per day over getting real Coke. I ended up spending the $100 for the entire shoot out-of-pocket to get my crew real soda and ended up with much happier folks.

4.2i Wardrobe, makeup, and hair

Good makeup artists also require some form of pay. They are far and few between, and very in demand. The skills required to do makeup for film are also very specific, and a great photo makeup artist may not know how to properly cover the blemishes on your actors' faces when shooting a movie. You can usually find decent to good people for $100 per day, and I would strongly recommend budgeting this much even if your film doesn't require any SFX makeup.

The makeup artist also serves an additional role: He or she is often the actors' confident, and having someone with solid people skills can help alleviate a lot of stress and tension on set. A good makeup artist will know how to reinforce the actors' confidence before he or she shoots a difficult take, and will often let the AD know when he or she realizes a cast member is having a difficult day.

Be aware of the number of cast members who will be on set on a given day and plan your makeup and hair crew accordingly. A very common way of starting your day two hours behind is to be understaffed in this department.

Wardrobe depends a lot on the type of film. Obviously if you're shooting a period piece you will need to budget accordingly for rentals. In most cases, for contemporary indie films you can work mostly with the cast's wardrobe and/or very inexpensive items acquired at thrift stores. In those cases you can usually find an unpaid or low-paid wardrobe supervisor. Again, this is a case where the promise of a nice credit (a front-end costume designer credit) will often do miracles to get someone smart and competent but with little film experience to work on a very small budget.

4.2j Transportation and locations

Transportation includes all costs related to getting people, materials, and equipment to and from the set, and includes parking. No matter how small the film I would allocate something to this department — which is often omitted on ultra-low budgets and inevitably, ends up coming out of the contingency fund.

If you are in a place that is not accessible by public transportation, you will have to cover gas for the cast and crew. If there is a fee for parking, the production will need to cover it. In large cities a college or university student or faculty member will generally be able to get you discounted access to blocking off entire side streets for crew parking for an entire day. This is a much better option in a lot of places than having to reimburse an entire crew for parking meters.

As mentioned in Chapter 3, locations are difficult to budget for, but keep in mind that if you spend a bit more on locations, you can save on set design.

4.3 Postproduction

Postproduction represents all costs associated with completing the picture once production has ended.

4.3a Editing

Let me say this loud and clear: After the director and the writer, the editor is the *third most important person* working on a film. The editor is called the second director because a good editor, short of making miracles happen, can salvage the movie from poor footage. Conversely, a bad editor can make a horrible film from excellent footage.

Experienced editors are rare and don't come cheap, but you can find talented young editors just out of school and want to make a name for themselves. This is definitely a post where you want to allocate some budget. I'd say try to save at least $5,000 at the lowest budget levels if possible. You may be lucky and find someone who will do the work cheaper and turn out to be good, like I did on a couple films, but keep in mind that editing a feature is a multi-month full-time job.

Your editor will probably spend more time working on the film than any other crewmember except the director and lead producer. With this in mind, you want to be able to pay the editor something if at all possible; otherwise, the person will likely have to work on the film during his or her spare time as he or she works on other projects to make a living, and your postproduction could go on for a long time. None of the other postproduction aspects can even start until you have a final, locked edit, so the editing speed will be critical to the eventual completion time of the film.

4.3b Color correction

Generally, on a small budget try to negotiate with your director of photography (DP) to do the color correction as part of his or her fee. Most

DPs will prefer this on smaller budgets anyway as they don't want an inexperienced color artist messing up their footage.

4.3c Visual effects

Try to budget at least a few hundred dollars on any film to be able to afford a few hours for a student to clean up blemishes and other imperfections once the film is complete.

4.3d Score

As opposed to other fields, there are plenty of composers out there who will have an interest in working on your film for free or cheap. This doesn't mean that you should try to get the most inexpensive artist if you can afford a better one. The score is obviously one of the very important components of a film, but it does give some flexibility if your budget can't support a normal fee (usually around $20,000 for scoring an entire low-budget film). If you spend the time looking, you can probably find the next emerging talent who will work on a couple films mostly for the experience.

4.3e Post-sound design and mixing

There's no getting around it, you will not get your film properly mixed and sound designed for less than $3,000 to $5,000 and should plan as such from the very early stages. Sound design and mixing is a very technical and involved job, and has little to no recognition in festivals unless you reach the Oscar level. Your best bet is to find a professional studio who supports independent films and will be willing to work at these rates if it likes your film and you give it the time to weave it into its busy schedule between other projects.

Call the studios in your area, pitch them your film and see what happens. Your next best bet is to go to the film schools and find a student or group of students who are willing to spend the time it takes for this type of fee in order to get a feature under their belt. Keep in mind, they will usually do this once or twice, then move on to normally paid projects.

4.4 Other costs

This category represents any additional general costs associated with making the film, such as insurance, legal fees, etc. It can also include marketing and film festival costs in some cases.

4.4a Insurance

Insurance is an incompressible cost of shooting a film. You may be tempted to skip it, but you shouldn't and most likely won't be able to. Even if you decided to shoot without insurance for cost-saving purposes (a terrible idea that leaves you exposed to massive lawsuits should anything happen on your set), if you hire SAG actors, you will be forced to show proof of insurance before they can work on your set. In a similar fashion, most locations will require liability insurance in order to grant you access.

The good news is that insurance can be relatively inexpensive when all is said and done. For less than $2,000 (still a large chunk of a $50,000 budget, but well worth it when you consider the benefits) you can generally get coverage for liability (i.e., damage to locations or injury caused to people not working on your set) for up to $1 million, a decent amount of equipment insurance (i.e., covers any damage to your camera or lighting gear), and workers' compensation (i.e., coverage of injuries sustained by your cast and crew). If you are really tight on budget, you will likely be able to avoid the latter as workers' compensation is generally not required by any party on a low-budget shoot, but I would recommend strongly that you get it. Should someone on your shoot get injured, you will then be liable to not only to cover his or her medical expenses, but also to damages awarded to the person if he or she chooses to sue the production.

One item to budget in addition to the cost of getting insurance coverage is the amount of the deductible, which is anywhere between $250 and $500. Also be aware that if you do any stunts or gun effects on set, you will need to purchase additional coverage, which can be expensive.

4.4b Legal

If you're on a tight budget, you can probably get away without any legal costs by using standard document templates for your deal memos and contracts.However, on a larger shoot, or if you decide to raise private funding, you will need to get a solid operating agreement done for your LLC, or at least reviewed by an attorney. (See Chapter 6 for more information about LLCs.)

Most major cities and filmmaking hubs in the United States do have not-for-profit organizations that are dedicated to providing legal resources to artists who can't afford to pay regular entertainment attorney rates. One such organization is Lawyers for the Creative Arts in

Chicago (http://www.law-arts.org/), one of the most genuinely helpful and useful entities I have found to assist filmmakers and other artists. When I needed a lawyer, this organization referred me to a great entertainment attorney who was nice enough to do the work on my three features on an entirely deferred basis (meaning he would only get paid if the films sold and made money). This is the best-case scenario, but with some research you can probably find an attorney who will be willing to work on a deferred or reduced basis if he or she likes you and your project.

4.4c Budgeting software

Even though a film budget can be sketched out in Microsoft Excel or any other spreadsheet software, it is recommended to use a dedicated software for it as it follows a very specific format. The industry standard is MovieMagic Budgeting (which also offers MovieMagic Scheduling). The software can be somewhat pricey, but again if you have a student or faculty member as the producer, he or she can get an educational license for a fraction of the retail cost.

4.4d The ever-evolving budget

Having given a broad overview of the structure of a budget, here is the most important note of all: Be prepared for your budget (and your schedule) to be constantly evolving, up until your last day of post-production.

Do not lock yourself into the numbers you see on paper at any stage, and be ready to keep rebalancing constantly. Some things you thought would cost nothing will end up representing large-line items, and some of the items you anticipated to be expensive might end up costing a fraction of what you thought.

Have your line producer update the budget daily with actual spent figures and keep reallocating and comparing to what you had planned. The trickiest thing about any production (and this includes very large budgets) is to have enough money left on the last few days of the shoot to make it happen. Countless productions run out of cash halfway through, and these films often don't get completed.

When I compare the first budget I drafted for *Chat* and the actual final amount spent, almost no line items are the same. We thought we'd work mostly with nonunion actors, but a vast majority of our cast ended up being SAG members. We thought we'd spend a fortune on getting a large office space for nine days, but we got it for free. Our insurance ended up being double what we planned, but we found a great caterer who saved us almost half our projected food budget.

The key is to know that if additional money needs to go to a department, money *has* to be taken from somewhere else. If you're lucky, these funds will already have been freed up by the time you need them. If you're not lucky, you may have to make tough choices; for example, do you prefer using live guns on set but killing a location you really wanted, or can you get away with using plastic guns and no squibs?

The key to successful budgeting is to over-budget every item at the start. Inevitably some or most line items will then end up less expensive than planned, which will then give you the leeway to allocate funds for unexpected expenses. Even on *Fall Away*, my initial budget was only $12,500 and most of my line items were in the single or double digits, I was trying to allocate 10 percent more than I thought things would cost. On *Roundabout American*, we consistently over-budgeted, and it gave us the ability to cover any surprises and even grant me a couple requests that had been initially denied.

A properly budgeted production will make for a smoother shoot, where the creative crew will be able to focus mostly on the art, rather than be worried about whether they will be able to afford the next day of shooting.

Fundraising

You have completed a preliminary budget, or even better, a few budgets at different levels that give you the flexibility to adapt to the amount of funding you can secure. Now it's time to find the funds to actually turn your project into reality.

Multiple tools are at your disposal. Just a few years ago, independent filmmakers were limited to presales or private investment to make their dreams come true. Nowadays, crowdfunding sites such as Kickstarter or Indiegogo provide new avenues for quickly raising the funds for a project.

Is one method better than the others? It depends on the amount of money you are looking for, whether your project can touch the hearts of a special interest group, and if you have someone famous associated with it. Crowdfunding sites like Kickstarter provide a great way to raise amounts ranging from a few thousand dollars to several hundred thousand. However, don't let yourself be fooled by the projects you see that raised large sums, and think that you will easily achieve the same result.

A Kickstarter campaign is a tedious, difficult process that for most people is adequate to raise a few thousand or, at best, a few tens of thousands of dollars. In order to go beyond that, you will likely need to have a "hook" (i.e., something that really holds mass appeal) or a name attached to your film. If the latter is true, presales will then become something to consider as well.

Presales consist of selling your film before it is made to a distributor who bets it will be able to recover the amount it advanced based on the cast you have. If you have no name actors, don't bother considering presales because you won't get them. Actors have to be "bankable" for a distributor to take the chance to advance money. Presales can also be costly and cumbersome, with a completion bond (i.e., a form of insurance that guarantees the distributor will see its money back if you can't complete the picture) being a requirement.

Private investors remain the most popular route for most filmmakers, and are usually the easiest path to aggregating budgets between $50,000 and $200,000 (and sometimes more).

A number of other tools exist, notably grants from the government or special interest groups that are usually geared at special interested projects.

1. Private Investors

Before the rise of crowdfunding, raising money from private investors was the most common way of funding smaller independent films. Recent changes to regulations have made this process easier than it used to be, and it remains a solid alternative to crowdfunding. Depending on your targeted budget and your connections, raising the funds from private investors might be the fastest way to raise the funds you need. On every film I made I got part or most of the money from private investors.

As mentioned previously, *Fall Away* initially had a $20,000 budget. At that time (2009) sites such as Kickstarter didn't exist, so private investment was the right road. The minimum investment amount was $5,000. Amongst the four producers we set out to find one investor each. This was a challenging time to raise funds, but we were still able to find four people who were willing to invest $5,000 in the film amongst our immediate circle.

Roundabout American had an initial budget of $1 million, an amount I could not realistically find within my immediate circle of possible investors. I decided to make the minimum investment amount $10,000, which meant I was looking for 100 people to complete my budget.

Tip: Don't split the investment into amounts so small that you'll need a large crowd of people because it becomes unmanageable. By the time you find all of them you will likely have lost half of the initial investors.

Because of the large sum required and the uncertainty I had of being able to collect the whole amount (and my narrow vision at the time that led me to believe that the $1 million budget was set in stone and the only way to get the film made), I felt it was fair to the investors to have them sign a two-year commitment and only collect the cash from them when the entire sum was found.

I started in 2008, and fairly quickly found 15 people who were willing to invest $10,000 each. Then the housing collapse hit, and the investor faucet dried up. By mid-2009 I was still stuck at my $150,000 level, unable to find a dime more. By mid-2010 when I decided I would make the film on a lower budget, I hit two major roadblocks.

First, my investors had committed to invest almost two years earlier, and some of them had seen their financial situation drastically change for the worst. Sure, they had signed a contract that committed them to releasing the funds, but practically speaking such a contract has little value. What was I going to do? Sue people for $10,000 who were practically broke and who are friends, or friends of friends? Had I collected the funds when they committed and put them on an escrow account, that account would have been earning interest for two years, and they would have had no way to back out (not to mention that their $10,000 would still exist and would eventually have gone into a film investment rather than disappear on the stock market).

Second, I had spelled out in the commitment paperwork that the $10,000 could only be invested if I raised at least $900,000 (90 percent of my $1 million budget). This was to give them the guarantee that I wouldn't just burn their money in an attempt to make the film on an impossible budget. What this meant was that when I decided to go ahead and make the film for $200,000 (or $150,000, if I really had to), technically every single one of my investors had the full right to back out because of the budget change.

I had learned from my experience on *Fall Away*. I knew I could make the film for much less, and I had partnered with a seasoned producer who could back me. It would be near impossible to go back to people I had looked in the eye two years before, and assure them that my experiences over these two years now made me confident I could get a quality film done for 20 percent of my original budget. Fortunately,

I convinced a good percentage that I could do it (and they were kind enough to support me despite the drastic change in direction) but I still lost about one-third of the people who had committed originally. I had to find ten new people to get to my $200,000.

On *Chat* I applied the lessons I had learned. I had four different budgets ready, and a solid argumentation to present to potential investors about the reasons the film would not suffer too much at the lower thresholds. I made the minimal investment amount $2,500 (we raised $22,500 from the Kickstarter campaign, so we only needed $25,000 to reach our second budget level of $50,000). I told my investors the film was happening at a set date no matter what and collected the funds right away once they committed. Between Kickstarter and private investors we raised the $50,000 we needed in about three months and were set to start shooting on time.

Your first step is to make a list of every person you know — whether they are close to you or you've only met them once. Next to these people write down the dollar amount you think they can reasonably invest in a film. This should represent your idea of an amount they can easily afford to lose without any harm to their overall financial situation. You don't want to find yourself in a position where you have made your friends invest their retirement savings or their kids' college fund in your movie. If you have some sort of moral framework, the responsibility is likely to prevent you from sleeping at night. Independent film is a very risky investment, where the chances of losing everything are substantially greater than the chances of making the money back.

There are legal constraints. Up until recently the Security and Exchange Commission (SEC) rules prohibited soliciting investments in the United States from individuals you did not have a direct preexisting relationship with, a relic from the stock market collapse of the 1930s. The *Jumpstart Our Business Startups Act* (*JOBS Act*) passed by congress in 2012 relaxes these rules quite a bit, allowing for "general solicitation" (i.e., reaching out to people you don't have a preexisting relationship with to consider an investment), and legalizing online crowdfunding investments (as opposed to donations only).

Make sure to review the legal requirements before signing on someone as an investor. The *JOBS Act* specifies a number of criteria must be met, geared at making certain the individual's net worth and/or income are aligned with the amount he or she is committing to your project.

Your next step is to consider the genre of your film when building the list. When I was raising money for *Fall Away* it had a strong LGBT component, the first people I pitched were friends who were either gay or sensitive to gay matters, as they would likely relate to the subject. A friend of mine made a film centered on the Jewish community in Chicago and tailored his fund-raising approach as such. Even if your film has no obvious connection to a given community, try to look below the surface to see if there may be an angle. *Roundabout American* was a broad comedy with no obvious angle, except for the fact that the lead character was French — 90 percent of the investors who funded the project ended up being French or with strong ties to France.

1.1 Create a pitch package

The pitch package usually consists of the following:

- Synopsis of the film (500 or so words, or one to two pages).

- Director's statement where the director describes his or her vision for the film.

- Key player bios, which is traditionally the director, producers, director of photography, if attached, and possibly the writer and composer.

- A few pages describing the investment structure and the marketing and distribution pitch for the film.

- Pictures or sketches, and a temp poster for the front cover. The more visual the better — you're pitching a film, a visual project. If you don't have any test footage, find royalty-free photos that relate to the themes and look and feel you're thinking of for the movie. If you have friends who can draw, ask them to sketch a few storyboards for important scenes in the film.

- Never send the script along with the initial query; a script is a significant time commitment to read and may discourage your investors from even considering the project.

Begin with your list of investors; the people who seem the most likely to invest the largest dollar amounts. The fewer investors the better as dealing with investors can be time consuming. Start with a phone call or an email, telling them you are working on a film project and querying whether they might be interested in considering a small investment. Attach the pitch package, ask them to review it, and propose to follow up within a week or two. You need to be persistent yet avoid being annoying.

Often you will find that your targeted investors are very busy people, who barely find the time to read the pitch package and may need several nudges in order to do so. Always ask whether it is OK to follow up within the given time frame. Include a deadline in your email; for example, "I will be completing the fund-raising round by February 24, and going to production on April 1." You know these deadlines are movable, but it's important to give a sense of urgency and let them know that the opportunity is finite in time; otherwise, you'll likely end up six months later waiting for responses.

A few days or weeks after you send the first few emails you will likely get some responses. These will come in three forms:

- Straight no. People who either don't want to invest in film or don't adhere at all to the concept you presented them.

- Might be interested. These people might ask for more information such as to read the script.

- Yes. This is a very rare case. You might get some people who will like you or the project enough to simply commit to an amount without even meeting you, especially if the minimal investment amount is a very small sum compared to their overall wealth.

Your final step is to physically meet the people who have shown interest, and close the pitch. What you will find is that anyone with some common sense will realize that an investment in a film is a way to support an artistic project that comes with a chance of recovering the invested amount rather than a traditional investment. In other words, they should fully expect to lose the amount they commit (and if they don't realize this, you need to be very clear and up front with them about it). What they will invest in is you if they believe you have the ability to complete the project and maybe build a career in the field; and possibly the project, especially if the film relates to a topic that is meaningful to them.

When pitching to people in-person, be concise, passionate, and honest. People will appreciate someone who is direct and gives them a clear picture of the shortcomings and risks the project may carry than someone who paints a picture that seems too good to be true.

Hopefully, after following the above steps you will see some commitments accumulate. In Chapter 6 we'll show you the next step, which is putting together a legal structure to carry the project.

2. Crowdfunding

The two most popular sites for crowdfunding are Kickstarter and Indiegogo. Choosing between the two can be tricky and depends on the project, and your confidence level that you will be able to reach your goal. Kickstarter forces you to reach your goal in order for you to collect the funds. This means that if you set a goal of $5,000 and only collect $4,500 in pledges, the whole campaign is canceled and the donors don't get charged. Indiegogo allows for campaigns where the proceeds will be collected whether the goal is reached or not.

We debated before settling on Kickstarter for *Chat*. On the one hand, the knowledge that you will be able to claim whatever people have pledged is comforting; on the other hand, the psychological pressure of knowing that nothing will come through if the goal is not met is a great incentive for the project creators to drive the fund-raising effort. More importantly, that pressure is also a great tool to push your potential donors. Once the goal is in sight, you have a very strong argument for asking people to donate more (or asking the first donors to up their ante) by letting them know that these final contributions will make or break everything. Also, knowing that the funds will be collected only if the requested amount is reached will likely inspire confidence in your donors that you will not find yourself in a position of trying to make the project happen with a fraction of the funding you really need.

Kickstarter is the leader in terms of notoriety and traffic, so if you feel that your goal is clearly achievable, it is the way to go. However, if you think your goal may be difficult to reach, and that you would have the ability to intelligently use the funds even if you only collect a percentage of the total you were aiming for, Indiegogo may be the better option.

In order to run a Kickstarter campaign you will have to create an Amazon merchant account, which is the payment processor Kickstarter uses. Kickstarter takes a fee of 5 percent of the amount raised. Amazon takes a fee that varies between 3 and 5 percent depending on the country and the amount raised. Indiegogo charges 4 percent for campaigns that reach their goal, and a whopping 9 percent for campaigns that don't, plus the same 3 to 5 percent for credit card payment processing. This means that you need to account for 8 to 14 percent of the funds raised going into fees.

In addition, neither service charges the donors' credit cards at the time of the pledge. The donors input their credit cards, but those only get processed once the campaign is complete. This means that inevitably you will run into a percentage that can range anywhere between 5 and 15 percent of credit cards that get declined for a variety of reasons. In that scenario, the donor is automatically contacted with a notification asking him or her to update his or her information. Plan for 5 percent of unfulfilled pledges.

Always set your campaign goal about 20 percent higher than what you want to actually collect. This will ensure that when all is said and done, you will end up with the amount you were seeking, or if you're lucky, even a tad more.

Another aspect to consider is taxation. Funds raised through the means of crowdfunding services are considered by the IRS to be taxable income. What this means is that if you run your crowdfunding campaign but don't spend that amount within the same fiscal year, you will have to pay taxes on the amount raised. Of course, this will be offset by losses incurred the following year when you actually spend the money, but by then you will already have paid the taxes, and will have been short that much money when shooting your film. There are some ways around this, but they are complicated, and you will need to seek the guidance of a professional accountant who is well-versed in these topics to circumvent this.

You should strongly consider timing your campaign so it ends at the *beginning* of the year during which you plan to produce your film. This will ensure that the production losses will offset the Kickstarter revenue so you are tax neutral by December 31.

2.1 Anatomy of a Kickstarter campaign that was funded

We raised $25,000 dollars on Kickstarter for our micro-budget film *Chat*. I wrote most of the copy for the Kickstarter campaign and I thought it might be helpful to break down what you'll need to write and what it might sound like in advance of you trying to raise cash for your own movie.

Note that our final tally was 197 backers and $25,456 pledged of our goal of $25,000. This was not 100 percent of our budget by any means, but it was a significant chunk. Without this $25,000, our project wouldn't have happened.

The following sections will give you some tips on how to get your Kickstarter campaign written, noticed, and funded.

2.1a Assemble a team

You need to find people who are invested, and who will not flake out. People who are realistic about the time they can commit and then deliver on their word. These people are the soldiers for your campaign. They will help build it and promote it.

2.1b Conceive the plan

It's in the earliest meetings that you'll divide responsibilities, establish a framework of expectations, and prepare the timetable to get things done. The video pitch has to be written and shot. The accompanying text pitch has to be written. The gifts for each price level have to be conceived, written, and probably rewritten. Then there's the little matter of brainstorming every living person you've ever known in preparation for a personalized email or Facebook message.

2.1c Video pitch

We had the idea that we would use a test scene we shot as a trailer for how the movie might look. It's a great looking scene (that cost all of $200 to shoot) and was an excellent teaser, but there was a problem. SAG issues ($800 for the use of a SAG actor) forced us to go a different way. I wrote a quick one-minute mini-scene in the tone of the story, followed by a 90-second director pitch given artfully by my ever-charming partner, Boris Wexler. We shot the video of the actress and her one-minute scene, plus the Boris material, in two days. Then we edited in whatever we could to make it visual (i.e., pickup street video with our 5D, stills from the script, and test scene) then edited everything into a three-minute pitch.

2.1d Text pitch

To accompany the video pitch you'll need the text pitch, which tells the world about the project, informs them what you're goals and dreams are, describes what their money might be used for, and gives a sense of the passion you're bringing for the project. Always show how passionately you feel for your material, why the story is unique and original, and how it can't be done without them. If you can't instill that passion into the text pitch, I'd suggest you set your goal low because you likely won't make it. This goes more toward setting realistic goals for how much money you can raise. Remember, you've got to make the full amount on Kickstarter or you get nothing.

The Story

Chat is a unique look inside a fragmented mind … the mind of Falcon. Falcon is photophobic, unable to handle light as you or I would, making his universe an alien landscape. Looking out with red-rimmed, hyper-sensitive eyes, he must break through his isolation and loss of human connection, and try to pull his daughter back from the brink. Seen through Falcon's distorted point-of-view, the film plunges the viewer into a "Lynchian" world of dizzying florescence, 15-watt lightbulbs, latex cat suits, and bad liposuction. Nothing is as it seems to be. Disturbing characters appear and disappear. Time and people fold back on themselves, leading to a bizarre story twist that you will never see coming, and that will change their world for keeps.

The Goal

We are raising money to begin production of our feature film, *CHAT*. We are hoping to begin production in Chicago this spring. If we reach our Kickstarter goal of $25,000 we will be well on the way to accomplishing this.

The director of *Chat*, Boris Wexler, has extensive experience in making low- and micro-budget projects. He brings with him not just experience, but multiple relationships made within the Chicago film community, experienced professionals who will work with us at a fraction of what their "market" rates are, thus adding tremendous value to the project — $25,000 might not seem like enough money to make a difference in the life of a movie, but it is!

Chat, we believe, is a movie you're going to be hearing about. It's a kick-ass story that will gain enough national attention for a theatrical release. We'd like it to be successful both in a commercial and artistic sense. We will submit to film fests around the country, also releasing it through social media on multiple VOD and streaming platforms.

The landscape of movie making has changed considerably in the last decade. We are now in a DIY (Do-It-Yourself) realm where technology has enabled nothing less than the democratization of cinema. A person who has never stepped foot on a movie set can pick up a Canon 7D and make a movie, and can bring his or her story to the screen. Digital filmmaking isn't the future; it's upon us, right now, which is the point of this Kickstarter campaign.

The only way a micro-budget movie gets made is with the support of friends and family. The goal through Kickstarter is to make this movie happen. You, who are reading this, are the key. You can help make this movie happen for as little as five dollars. Pledge a donation. Please join our team.

Where the Money Will Go

Our goal is to raise a minimum of $25,000 for this project. After the film is completed, we plan on submitting it to film festivals around the world. Anything raised above our minimum goal will go directly into the production of *Chat*. Here is how we intend to use the funds raised:

- Increase the quality of all production concerns including the actors, key production staff, crew, and locations.

- Help offset unforeseen additional production costs.

- Manufacturing costs for backer rewards (Blu-rays, print materials, etc.).

- Digital distribution costs for backers downloading the film.

- Festival submission fees.

The funds we're hoping to raise are only a part of the budget and will allow us to cover the assets we have yet to finance. The entire production has been budgeted and scheduled from start to finish. We know what it is going to take to bring this film to its audience. We need you to help us carve out as much shooting time as possible. Thanks to Kickstarter, we have a way to connect directly to our audience. You can help us create a story that would otherwise have no way to get off the ground. And because we're making a smaller movie without a big studio overhead, we can finish it for a hundredth of the cost of a Hollywood blockbuster, in a fraction of the time, and deliver it directly to you.

We welcome your input. Backers of the project will be given access to a private online community where they can watch the progress of the film through updates and behind-the-scenes video, and to communicate with the filmmakers personally on an exclusive forum. Our goal is to be open and honest about making the movie we love and sharing it with our supporters as we go along.

$25,000 is an ambitious amount of money to raise, but *Chat* is an ambitious film. Even with everyone working at reduced rates or for free, we still have a lot of hard costs over a 15-day shoot, including crew, props, locations, and equipment rentals. After factoring in Kickstarter fees, credit card processing, and rewards, we will need every penny raised here to make this movie happen.

We plan to shoot the film in March and April, and to begin editing over the summer. We have a goal of being done by September, 2013. Then we will start submitting the film to festivals. Most people won't see the film until 2014. Your pledge assures that you will be the first to see the film, at least six-months before everyone else.

Why We're Doing This

Chat is a passion project. It began for writer Paul Peditto as an adaptation of a stage play based on a true story. *Chat* is a movie that might never see the light of day in the Hollywood system dominated by remakes, sequels, and branded tent-pole entertainment. With DIY filmmaking technologies in digital cameras, powerful editing and production software tools, and a willingness of the Chicago filmmaking community to support projects of worth — *Chat* will have a chance to see the light of day. This is not about getting rich, or becoming famous. It's about putting a personal vision on the screen — something that moves from personal experience into the universal, something that resonates with an audience. To make a movie that matters. Thanks for helping us with this mission.

2.1e Gifts

The gifts section is a tricky one to write. For each accompanying price level the donors should get a prize. You'll need to pick a price point to start awarding gifts (Kickstarter allows $1 contributions; we started our gifts at the $10 range). Traditional gifts of DVDs, T-shirts, posters, and a mention in the credit roll or on IMDB. Find a way to be creative in gift giving that speaks specifically of your project.

Chat is about adult Internet chat so the gifts were racy. For instance at $100, the gift was a sexy voicemail from the lead actress. For $250, the gift was a prop from the movie. For $750, the gift gave donors on the set as a walk-on extra part, or allowed them to name the pet mouse of the lead character. You want to make it as interactive as possible. Get them rooting for you by involving them in decisions such as picking the poster or character names. Make them feel like they're a part of the project, not just a $20 donation.

Your gifts should be suited to the genre. For example, funny gifts if you're making a comedy. Cyber-sex-themed if you're making a flick, like we were, set in an online XXX chat room. You've got to use your imagination when creating gifts. The trick is to bring your audience in on your process immediately. Get them cheering for you to be funded, get them talking about you on social media sites. Generate a buzz ASAP.

The following show you a few examples of what we did for *Chat* gifts.

Bad Kitty

$10 — Little Orphan Annie and her sexy cam model friends will welcome you to the world of *Chat* by posting your name on Facebook and Twitter, and on the donor sections of our upcoming website.

Angels with Dirty Faces

$20 — Get a private link for an exclusive look at a scene from the movie *Chat*. Disclaimer: Annie will not be baking blueberry muffins or strawberry shortcake.

Heels, Pearls, and Black Boots

$25 — Get everything listed above, plus a free download of an HD digital copy of the finished film.

Latex and Lace

$50 — Everything listed above, plus access to exclusive behind-the-scenes footage as we make the film.

Ruby Red Lipstick

$75 — All of the above in addition to a DVD of the finished film, an awesomely designed T-shirt, and a signed 117 film poster.

Victoria's Secret

$100 — A gift for the writers out there … A Blu-ray instead of a DVD plus everything listed above and a signed copy of the script, including script coverage from the writer, Paul Peditto.

Voulez-vous?

$250 (only 3 slots available) — Born in France, Annie will whisper sweet nothings from the language of love in your ear with a personalized voice message. Also includes a "Thank You" credit in the film's ending credits and on IMDB.

Black Silk Panties

$250 — Not sure what prop you'll be sent, but it'll come in a brown paper wrapper!

The Cat's Meow

$500 — A purrfect package for the writers of crazed, kick-ass thrillers … Two tickets to the premiere, a signed photo with the director (if you attend the premiere), and a private, one-hour script consultation with Paul Peditto.

Mickey Mouse, He's Not

$750 — That's right, you get to name a character! The one and only pet mouse of our lead character Falcon! Plus a private custom video from Annie, a 246 high-gloss poster of the film signed by key cast and crew.

Naughty, Naughty!

$1,000 — You'll receive four tickets to the movie's premiere, and a featured extra spot in the film for you or someone of your choice (transportation and lodging not included).

Bitchin', Awesome, and Rad

$1,500 — You'll be the after-party sensation … This is the $750 package plus 10 tickets to the movie's premiere and after party and one day of unlimited set access (transportation and lodging not included).

Angel from Heaven

$2,500 — A shimmering moon or five-color sunset is beautiful, but not more beautiful than *Chat Goddess Annie*, and you're having dinner with her! Get the $1,000 package plus a private dinner with a lead cast member, the director or the producer, or all of the above! (Transportation and lodging not included.)

Camageddon!

$5,000 — Your name echoing across the digital divide. You'll get the $1,500 package plus an Associate Producer credit on screen and IMDb, including an all-access-set VIP pass and 20 tickets to the movie's premiere.

Wall of Fame Legend

$7,500 — Become an instant legend of DIY filmmaking … The Executive producer head credit on screen and IMDB (instead of AP credit), plus you'll be able to view and critique preliminary cuts of the film.

2.1f Personalize email

The personalized email is the most important part of the entire process. You need to go from A to Z on your Google Gmail list and write a personal letter to every person who might donate. No, you cannot write a form letter and mass mail it! You must personalize the email so that you are speaking specifically to each person you ask.

You have an inner circle that must come through as backers of your project. This process will take hours upon hours but should give you a good base toward attaining your goal. Ask friends and family first; get the Kickstarter campaign off to a fast start with Mom's money in the first 48 hours, then work toward good friends, then to decent friends, acquaintances, and then the gas station attendant who struck up a conversation with you last Christmas!

2.1g Social media

Needless to say you're going on Facebook for this campaign. You must. You need to find a balance between awareness and spam. I posted a message once a day, which planted our movie idea with other people who then linked to our campaign and broadcast it themselves. If your friends are broke, they can still help by spreading awareness.

The more your project is out there on multiple social media platforms, obviously, the better. The goal is to bring in that mythical creature into your project — the "lurker." Someone no one on your team knows. Kickstarter admits that the vast majority of money raised is directly through friends and family, but occasionally if the campaign is visually compelling or strikes a chord, you will get people you don't know to contribute. If the first 30 seconds of your video isn't visually compelling, you can pretty much kiss off any lurker money.

2.1h Updates

It's standard knowledge that updates are critical. Stay in touch with your donors. Let them know what's happening with the project. Keep them abreast on the progress with the goal, maybe new talent or locations found. Develop an emotional bond, have them rooting for the project to happen.

You *must* do project updates if the campaign is funded. The people who donate want to be a part of the movie-making process, so help them by giving them timely updates on what's happening through the preproduction, production, and postproduction processes. Most importantly, make sure you deliver on the gifts you promised.

Legal and Tax Aspects

In order to make the film and accept the investments you will need to create a production company. It is generally recommended to make a single company for each separate project, for multiple reasons, which will be discussed in this chapter. We also explain the benefits of tax credits.

1. Creating the Legal Entity and Structuring the Investments

First, you want to limit the liability on a per project basis. For example, you make a film and everything goes great, but on your next film someone gets severely injured on set and sues the production company for negligence. You don't want your first project to be impacted by a lawsuit, which will likely have serious financial consequences. If you have two production companies, anything negative tied to one film will not impact the other.

Second, you are likely to have different investors with a different equity allocation from project to project. Keeping multiple companies allows you to structure each deal as makes the most sense.

How is an independent film deal structured? Generally, the capital of the production company gets split between two groups — the investors and the producers. The investors are people who generally contribute cash or valued goods to the film. In return for their investment, they get a share in the production company, which gives them claim to a percentage of the revenue. Investors generally don't have voting rights —meaning they don't have a say in the practical decisions around the production.

The "producers" don't necessarily include just the producers, but anyone who is associated to the production and contributes their work instead of cash. On almost all my films I have chosen to include several lead crewmembers in the producers' group — either as a substitution for part or total of their cash compensation, or as a thank you for people who did a great job and went above and beyond.

The investors usually have claim on all the revenue to the film exclusively until their investment is reimbursed. Sometimes the deal calls for greater than 100 percent before the revenue gets split between investors and producers, in order to ensure the investors will see some profit. A general rule of thumb is to give the investors 50 percent of the shares in the company, though this number can be less on lower budgets.

Using *Roundabout American* as an example:

- The investors received 50 percent of the shares in the film for their collective $195,000 investment.

- The producers kept the other 50 percent, split mostly between myself and Julian Grant, the line producer, the editor, the director of photography, and the composer.

- The investors were to receive 100 percent of the revenue until 140 percent of their investment was reimbursed. Then the subsequent revenue would be split between investors and producers.

This structure is flexible. On *Fall Away* and *Chat*, the investors received less than 50 percent of the shares, the reasoning being that our ability to make the film happen on such small budgets relied essentially on crewmembers forfeiting pay; hence, calling for a larger percentage of shares to be allocated to the "producers" (which included key crewmembers). On *Fall Away* the investors received a 20 percent stake for a $20,000 investment. On *Chat* they received a roughly 25 percent stake for a $50,000 investment. In the end these numbers were somewhat arbitrary, and the result of case-by-case negotiation and a sense of what felt fair on a per-project basis.

The vehicle most used for independent films is a Limited Liability Company (LLC). The LLC is a structure that allows multiple partners to come together and benefit from taxation that is similar to a partnership while being afforded limited liability. An LLC is a lighter structure than a corporation, with less paperwork and requirements, and a more straightforward taxation mechanism. LLCs generally cost a bit more to create than corporations, but have a much lower yearly maintenance cost.

Once you have formed your LLC, you will need an operating agreement, which will regiment the relationship between shareholders, and a set of subscription documents for your investors. Although templates are generally available online, it is strongly recommended to consult an attorney to, at the very least, review the documents before signing them and presenting them to shareholders.

2. Tax Credits

Many areas in both the United States and Canada offer tax incentives geared at encouraging filmmakers to shoot in those states or provinces. These tax credits can then usually be sold for cash during the year production takes place to other corporations that can effectively use them to offset profits, and the money can be used for postproduction or marketing.

Here's a simple example: Say you have a $200,000 budget for your film. In Illinois the minimum requirement to claim the credit is $100,000 on Illinois salaries, goods, and services (meaning anything out of state will be excluded). Now let's imagine that your budget includes $150,000 for production and $50,000 for postproduction and marketing. Out of the $150,000 for production, $120,000 will be spent in Illinois and the rest elsewhere, and the entire postproduction budget will be spent in Illinois.

You are now faced with two choices. You can only claim the credit once per production. This means that if you claim the tax credit at the end of the shoot but before postproduction starts, you will only be able to apply the credit to the amounts spent so far ($120,000). The Illinois tax credit is 30 percent, which means you will recover a sizeable $36,000 from your $120,000 —enough to cover most of your post. However, if you waited until postproduction is complete, you could now claim the credit on $170,000, giving you $51,000 back to spend on marketing, reimburse your investors, or pay deferred compensations you negotiated with your crew in light of your plan to claim a tax credit.

Obviously the preferred choice is to wait until the film is complete in order to claim the full amount, but realistically you may be better off spending the money you have on production to make the best film possible, then use the tax credit to pay for post.

From a practical standpoint, my experience with the tax credit is that it can be a very tedious and drawn out process, but it's well worth it.

The record keeping required for a tax credit application needs to be exhaustive to say the least. Every single receipt needs to be kept, along with justifications against the budget and proof that the money was indeed spent in Illinois. No exceptions. Again, I speak of Illinois because it is my experience, but the process is just as regimented in other states and Canadian provinces.

You will need to hire a certified accountant accredited by the local film office to certify the books and submit the application. The accountant's fee can range anywhere between $5,000 and $10,000 so you will need to include this in the budget. Note that some accountants will wait for the tax credit funds to come in before they get paid.

Generally, once production is over, you can account for one or two months at best before being able to submit the application. Once the application is in, the processing can take up to six months, usually with a lot of back and forth of additional information being requested.

At the end of the six months, if all goes well, you will receive a paper to be used as credit against taxes to be paid on profits. The problem is, you don't have any profits to report, and likely won't have any for a while, until the film is sold and the initial investment has been recouped. Luckily, the tax credit is transferable, which means you can sell it for cash to other firms that have an actual use for it during the current fiscal year. In order to do this, you will have to go through a tax credit broker (usually listed on the local film office's website, or recommended by the CPA), who will find a match between your project and a firm that wants to acquire the credit, usually for 90 cents on the dollar. That process can go very quickly as it did on *Roundabout American*; we sold ours within a week.

When all is said and done, the tax credit, despite all the headaches that come with it, is a great initiative, and a solid way to finance your postproduction costs.

Casting

The decisions made in casting will go a long way to deciding what the very success of your movie will be. Note that writer doesn't make the final call on who is cast. Not unless the writer happens to be the director and/or producer, which almost never happens on a studio movie, and rarely on a $10 million or more budgeted Indie.

The casting priority pyramid parallels the final cut pyramid for Hollywood movies. Directors make final casting decisions. If you're the writer, you won't be in the loop on final casting decisions.

Micro-budget, of course, changes the dynamic. Chances are good that if you're a micro-budget writer you're also either the director and/ or producer. That means you're not only in the room, but you might actually be the one deciding who gets hired.

With *Jane Doe*, we had $250,000, giving us indie-level money that brought us a big-time New York casting agent, Marcia Shulman. She came in when my producer brother got the bright idea to leverage a powerful casting agent by promising a producer role (a strategy he used to get Paul Dano to act in his micro-budget film, *Light and the Sufferer*, see the download kit for more details). We had $250,000, a strong script, then Marcia came in giving us access to Gersch Agency, Paradigm Talent Agency, and APA, which gave us access to many great actors such as Calista Flockhart, Edie Falco, and Vinny Pastore. Life is great when there's indie money.

But what happens when you've got $44,000 total? Choices happen. Up front, concerning casting, you'll start with this: Name actor or not? You can write a two-day cameo that can be played by, most likely, a B-name actor who you will pay his or her rate. In doing so, the actor will loan his or her name to your movie. Paying them his or her rate for one or two days won't bankrupt you and, possibly, the person will take less money for back-end participation. Point being, you will pay up-front money for a name that should help on the back end with film festivals and distributors. Doesn't take a genius to know that your chances of landing distribution go up with a name actor.

The other option, much more common, is to go the "no-name" route. Cast the best local actor you can find. Make the best movie you can with the resources you have. Plenty of movies make the Sundance Film Festival with no-name actors. A not-so-well-known fact is that agents must inform their clients of any viable offer, which in turn increases your odds that the actor might actually read the script, which in turn increases your odds (from zero) that they might be intrigued to take on your micro-budget for the pittance you're offering up-front if you juice-up back-end profit participation. It's worth a shot!

1. Where to Find Actors

This leads to another decision: Even if you go with no names, you still need to decide if you're going with SAG or non-SAG actors. There's no one-size-fits-all advice I can give here. My situation in Chicago will not be yours in Omaha. While there isn't much production money originating in Chicago, but there is a stunning talent pool of actors. It begins in the drama schools of colleges such as DePaul, Art Institute of Chicago, and Columbia College; and continues with the astounding theater scene. Throw in the five TV shows currently producing in Chicago and you get the idea. Chicago is loaded. My odds of finding good non-SAG actors goes through the roof here.

This is the reason you want to control micro-budget costs at script level. If you can limit the key actors to a limited number of days, it increases the chances you can make SAG's low-budget $125-a-day offers to key actors.

To find actors, you can post on Breakdown Express (https://www.breakdownexpress.com/), make calls to local casting agents, put up notices at local acting schools, call local theaters, and yes, try Craigslist.

2. Auditions

If you're the writer of a studio or indie flick, you likely won't get within sniffing distance of final casting decisions. That's reserved for the money people and director. Or, if you're a hyphen guy (i.e., writer-director) and your last name is Kaufmann, Tarantino, or Black.

The dynamic shifts with the micro-budget. You'll be in the room. That's because in addition to being the writer, you're likely the director and/or producer.

For *Jane Doe*, I found myself giving smiley faces, half-smiley faces, or frowny faces to the actors after their auditions. Yes, seriously. Don't give smiley faces, OK? Instead, set up your room this way:

- Reserve a space where the actor performances won't disturb anyone, and where you won't be disturbed. You should practice the pay-for-nothing-if-possible when trying to find space for auditions. For example, I book rooms through Columbia College because I work there.

- Create a welcome area outside with a table and chairs. On the table will be the "sides" (scenes for each actor). The actors will check in, be given sides, and have been scheduled with enough time in between auditions (e.g., 10 to 15 minutes) to look over the sides and prepare.

- Record the auditions. You'll have a single long table with the director, producers, and/or writer. Actors will come in, be greeted by the director, drop off a résumé, be asked if they have any questions by the director, and begin the audition. They'll be asked to read, either with someone from the movie (reading a role from the table) or with another actor in the callbacks. They'll then be thanked and exit. The next actor will be shown in — rinse, lather, and repeat.

You may have noticed that the audition is the director's show. The director is in charge, both of the process of the audition and the results. Unless, as a condition of his or her being hired the producers have control, it will be the director's call who is ultimately cast. That said, if your director is Captain Bligh from *Mutiny on the Bounty* in the audition room, there's a good likelihood he'll be a power tripper on set, and you might take note of that. Only a fool wouldn't consult the other people in the room on who to call back or not. When the actor leaves the room it's not uncommon for the director to look around the table and ask for brief thoughts on each actor. It will help determine who you call back.

As mentioned in the list above, record the auditions. It's a curious thing, but sometimes the strongest actor in the room, isn't. Meaning: This is film. Well, digital. Actor's performances have a tendency to look different in the camera than in person. Occasionally the person who you thought was in the room comes off as stilted. The person you thought was stiff comes off as subtle and intriguing.

Review the audition tapes you like and consult your people. Create a list for each role and the actors you want to call back. Make those calls and book the callbacks. You'll need a Casting Director to do all this tedious groundwork.If it's micro-budget, guess who probably ends up getting this job? You. And guess what it pays: Yep. $0.

3. Callbacks

The callbacks are a different animal from the initial general auditions. These are narrowed-down to your best actor options. You'll likely be pairing actors (and will want to schedule for that). These characters have several scenes together and you'll want to see the chemistry the actors have together. You also want to see how the actors take directions and do follow-up readings. It's far more impressive for an actor with no preparation to take his or her reading in a whole different direction than just repeating his or her first "choice."

Never forget, whoever you hire, you'll be spending days, if not weeks with that person on set. The audition process is an audition for the actor-director relationship as well. You don't want to be shackled to an arrogant, inflexible diva for 18 days. Especially not on a micro-budget where everyone will be asked to go above and beyond in terms of energy and commitment. Look for the actor who will bring you these intangibles.

The great strength of Boris is his pragmatism. He believes in an empirical approach. Yes, he trusts his gut, but he also wants to know what the people around him are thinking. In Chat, when it came time to make the final choice for one of the lead characters, Boris decided on Actor A. He asked me and the producers who watched the callbacks who they would choose. It was a clean sweep for Actor B. Boris cast Actor B. That is a very great strength and something you should endeavor to emulate in your own micro-budget experience.

Tip: Trust your gut on casting, but keep an open mind.

Postproduction

Postproduction can be both one of the most exciting and one of the most nerve-racking stages of making a film. On the one hand, you've spent all this time prepping and shooting, finally you have the material in the can, and can't wait to see it all come together. On the other hand, this is where you discover all the mistakes, the "what ifs" and the things you could have done better. It is also by far the longest part of the process (at least for independent films). Postproduction is usually done in five distinct steps, which are described in this chapter.

1. Editing

On *Roundabout American* I had chosen to edit fast in order to meet some festival deadlines that were dear to me, notably Cannes. I had my editor cut the film week after week as we were shooting in order to get to an assembly cut (i.e., the very first stage of the edit — a very rough assembly of scenes in script order) shortly after the shoot was over. We then completed the rest of the edit in three months of time.

One of the biggest incentives to complete the edit as fast as possible is the fact that this process holds up the rest of postproduction.

While sound design, visual effects, score, and color corrections can all take place at the same time, none of it can happen until the edit is locked. The reason being is that all these actions are timed to the edit. In other words, if a sound designer tries to design sound for a scene and then the edit changes, the sound department will effectively have wasted most of its time, and will have to restart from scratch as none its work will sync up to the final edit. Same thing goes for the other departments.

The biggest reason not to rush the edit is that it's the most important part of the postproduction process, and one of the most critical pieces of making a film. The edit is what binds all the work that has been done before. A good editor can salvage entire scenes where the acting is uneven, bring the slow pieces of a script to life by trimming and adjusting intelligently, and sometimes even change the way the story is told. The same images shown in a different order can tell a totally different story.

A very famous experiment, the Kuleshov Effect, illustrated this by showing an audience three assemblies of shots, and asking them questions afterwards. The first cut showed a close-up of a pensive man, then a coffin. The second cut showed a close-up of a pensive man as well, then a bowl of soup. The third showed again a pensive man, then a pretty woman lying on a couch. When asked what the man's expression reflected in each case, the audience answered sadness in the first scenario, hunger in the second, and lust in the third — in each case saying his performance was great. What they didn't realize was that the shot of the pensive man was the same exact one in all three cuts. The power of editing had made an expressionless actor create an emotion.

On *Chat* I decided not to rush the edit, and to take the time that was necessary to get the best film I possibly could. I sat down with my editor, Erin, for the first time a few weeks after the shoot was over — giving her time to assemble the first few reels. I usually cut up features into ten-minute reels, in order to facilitate the process. The editing software (in this case Final Cut Pro for Mac) handles ten-minute bits easier than it does a full-length one-hour film.

Cutting the film in reels also allows for flexibility when the time comes to turn it over to the other departments, as you can lock individual reels rather than the entire picture. For example, if you're still working on some details of the opening and end of the film, but the middle part is done, you can save some precious time by getting the reels that are finished to sound and to the composer while taking your time to continue polishing the parts that need it.

On the first pass, Erin and I would work once a week, cutting a reel a week. She would have a reel assembled before I got there, we would review it and make edits, then she would polish it for the following week as well as assemble the following reel. During this very first rough pass, I usually try not to worry too much about details, and rather find the rhythm of each scene. How fast should the cut go by? What are the important moments? Where should the focus go? This first pass also allows for identifying potential problems such as missing footage, potential pickups that could be needed, etc. The goal here is to put the film together, get a feel for it as a complete product, and then refine it.

During this initial stage I only sought feedback from Paul and my producers Lucy and Jessica, and requested general notes: Does this scene work as a whole? Does the pacing seem mostly correct? Once we went through this rough-cut process and had an assembled film, I sent the link to a few people I trust and are knowledgeable about the editing process and the filmmaking process in general to get some more opinions. Again, I was just asking for very general feedback before proceeding.

The next stage, known as the "fine cut," involves going through the reels again, this time paying even more attention to detail. The goal is to get a first copy in order to gather more feedback and do a test screening before moving on to the last stage, which is the "final cut."

When moving through the fine cut we were able to go slightly faster — two reels a week. At that point we're looking at fine details, how the cuts match each other, does the cutting style advance the story and emotions the scene is trying to convey? I strongly recommend laying a temporary score under key scenes, especially if they are action-based as opposed to dialogue heavy. Music is the only way to pace scenes, and pasting a score will help both the editing and the feedback-collection process when shown to a test audience.

Once the fine cut is assembled, I hold a test screening in front of an audience of a few dozen people. I also send the cut for detailed notes to people I trust who are willing to spend the time to give time-code notes to an entire cut.

There are multiple benefits to holding a screening in front of a live audience. First, it allows me as the director to actually sit in a room full of people who are watching the film. By that stage I'm usually so desensitized to the film that it becomes difficult to feel any emotion or really sense what works and what doesn't. Having seen a project unfold from start to finish means that you've heard the same lines over and over — from reading the script, rehearsing with actors, then doing take after take after take on set, and finally by sitting with your editor over two iterations of a cut. By this point you can recite every line in the entire film top to bottom, but are clueless to know whether a scene actually works.

Even though written notes will give you precise and insightful feedback, they don't compare to the emotion you can gather from a crowd watching the film. If it's a comedy, you will instantly know what scenes are funny or not and when or where people laugh. If it's a drama, you will sense the tension in the room and by looking at the viewers' faces you can gather a large amount of intuitive information.

I usually follow the screening with a question and answer session where I ask the audience a number of pointed questions. Again, nothing beats the spontaneity of people who just watched the film responding on the spot. It's also an easy way to gather a show of hands on questions you might have, or points where the director and producer disagree.

Usually, with a quality fine cut, the process to go to a final cut is smooth. The screenings give you good information as to what scenes should be cut, if any, and the detailed notes aggregated will give you insight that should lead to a few weeks of fine-tuning before ending up with a final product. For *Chat*, that turned out not to be the case.

Even though Erin and I were happy with our fine cut, our test screenings clearly showed that a film is more than just the sum of its parts. Despite everyone complimenting us on the quality and professionalism of the edit and agreed that scenes mostly worked one at a time, a couple of major structural notes were made. The first two-thirds of the film were way too slow. The first five minutes were unengaging. In addition, the plot twists were not set up well enough, which led to a very abrupt shift halfway through the film.

Interestingly, Paul and I had been arguing over a number of scenes to try and figure out if they worked or not. Paul wanted to cut some scenes, I wanted to cut others. We thought this was the main point of contention. The audience made us both right (though I won with a light edge), and generally said there was no issues with the scenes themselves. It was the overall pacing of the film that failed, and the way the story was set up.

The following week Erin and I sat down to start what would become the longest final cut editing process I ever went through — almost four months of reshaping when we expected four weeks. We had to go through the film again, but instead of working scene by scene we worked section by section. We cut up scenes that were long and split them in two parts. We didn't eliminate any scenes, but performed heavy dialogue trims on quite a few of them. Then came the biggest problem — the first five minutes. At this late date, what could we do?

With our production budget depleted, we had no way to reshoot a new beginning. We decided to use a gimmick seen in many films — start the film by giving the viewer an insight into what happens later in the film. You take a character who goes from A (a good spot) to Z (the horrible place he ends up in at the end of the film), and show the viewer at the beginning of the film a glimpse of the moment that would equate to the letter X (where the hero is already doing poorly, but you're not giving up the ending). Then you cut the scene to show what the character's thinking at that point and flash through select moments in the film that hint at the upcoming disaster that takes place two-thirds into the film.

If the effort is successful, we would have solved both issues the test audiences expressed. First we would have created tension that would sustain the viewer while the tension develops at the beginning of the film. They know something bad is going to happen, they've had a glimpse of it, and now rather than watching a man searching for his lost daughter, they are wondering how he will get to the point they saw in the new intro. Second, through an intelligent assembly of imagery we would have hinted at the upcoming plot twist — just enough to let the viewer know that there is one coming, but without revealing what the twist really is. When the twist actually does happen, the audience will then feel less cheated and will remember that moment at the very beginning.

In the midst of this process, we started picking out the reels that seemed easiest, locking them, and shipping them to sound and color correction in order to save time. What this means is that by the time we looked at the complete edited product, we had a number of reels we just couldn't make any changes to anymore without upsetting the entire postproduction process. In an ideal world we would have waited, but we had some imperatives that forced us to move forward.

A lot of people will request more feedback on the final cut. I don't. By that stage I generally have a clear idea of what I'm looking for and the solutions I want to put in place. Someone Paul and I know told us while we were gathering extensive feedback on the fine cut and trying to balance and weigh the feedback of multiple people that I was "directing by committee." I don't agree with that. Film is an art form defined by collaboration. Getting feedback from people you trust and respect can only be helpful.

At the end of the day it's the director who makes final artistic decisions. Paul sent one last email emphasizing some of the decisions I made he disagreed with, I had read and considered every note he'd gave (and had taken about 75 percent of his notes), but in the end it was my final decision as direction that stood, and Paul respected that.

2. Scoring the Film

Working with a composer has always been one of the most interesting aspects for me; mostly because it's the area I'm the least knowledgeable about. If I had to make a film without any help, I could probably write not too awful, shoot the whole thing, and make it look acceptable, edit it, even do some basic sound design. However, I'd be clueless even trying to compose three notes of the original score. I don't have any musical background, and zero musical ear; I'm the worst singer anyone ever met — even Happy Birthday comes out lousy!

I was lucky enough to work on my last two films with a composer I met through a common friend, and whose sensibilities I can rely on, Robert Palos. Because of my lack of technical musical knowledge, we discuss things in simple terms. Once Robert reads the script, he starts asking me questions about genres I envision. For *Chat*, I told him right off the bat I saw electronic music. I sent him a couple pieces of music Paul and I liked, and he started writing some tunes.

Though the actual score timing can't really start until you have a final cut, the composer can often put together melodies as early as the rough-cut stage. Because of the low budget of the film, Robert was singlehandedly composing and performing from home using software called Logic Pro. For the first couple months, while we were working on the rough cut, he mostly tried to find the main melodies for the film. He'd sent me ideas, with scenes he thought they might be good for, and I'd basically tell him whether I liked them or not. We would mostly communicate in terms of "mood" or "color" for given scenes or moments.

The benefit of this process is that by the time we had a fine cut, we had an array of semi-cohesive pieces of score we could lay under the scenes to see how they worked, rather than using a score from other films to be replaced at a later time. The downside was on Robert's end, as the process was longer for him and more tedious than if he had worked with a director who could better express what type of music he was looking for.

Once the final cut is locked, you identify which scenes you want scored. Dialogue scenes are tricky; it can be hard to gauge whether a scene will require music until the edit is completed. Some scenes I initially thought would not require score ended up desperately needing it; often to help cover performance or editing glitches that are sometimes unavoidable with the footage that is available. Other scenes you thought you needed to score might not require it because the performance is strong. In that case, music would detract from it.

Score is one of the most subjective portions of the filmmaking process. Even though sensibilities vary on every aspect, people will usually recognize a good story even if they don't like it. They may hate an actor, but acknowledge his performance is great. They might think your film should have a blue palette instead of a warm one, but will still see it's well shot.

With music, I've found that even people whose opinion I respect tend to be unable to move away from their subjective point of view, and will tend to have extremely strong personal opinions. Because of this, music is one element where I usually don't ask for feedback. I may not be musically gifted, but I trust my taste enough to know if a piece is good or not, and I trust Robert enough for him and I to come to conclusions on score without much additional input.

Once all the score is assembled, the composer needs to mix it, and deliver grouped instrument tracks to the sound mixer for final integration into the soundtrack. That part can take place right before the actual mixing process, giving the composer the time to work in parallel with sound design and mixing once the edit is completed.

3. Sound Design

Sound design is one of the most critical parts of postproduction, and often tends to be rushed on independent films as it's the very last piece to be completed and tends to often find itself racing against the deadline of a cast and crew or similar screening.

My experience with sound design on the two features that I directed was vastly different. On *Roundabout American*, the sound design and mixing process was done by one person, an extremely talented and committed recent graduate of DePaul University. Rob worked day and night for more than six months to get it done, and completed a job that is usually done by an entire team all on his own, including putting on high heels to record foley for our leading actress. The end result was good, but the time it took ended up being the bulk of postproduction, and the toll it took on Rob (who worked for 86 hours straight the week of the cast and crew screening surviving on Red Bull in order to turn in the final mix) made it a risky endeavor.

On *Chat* I was lucky enough to find a professional Chicago-based sound studio, Noise Floor, that liked the project enough to accommodate the low budget of the production. We got a full team to work on it, and the entire process took less than three months (and would have been shorter had we not been delayed on the editing side). In both cases, here's how the process broke down.

Initial sound spotting: Once you have a fine cut assembled, the director gets together with the lead sound designer to watch the film, and discuss in broad strokes what the main sound-design elements will be, scene by scene. This process also allows spotting immediate production sound issues, in order to identify scenes that may need to be ADR'd (ADR stands for Automated Dialogue Replacement, or the process of dubbing certain scenes after they are shot if the sound captured on location is deficient or not usable in post).

Once initial sound spotting is done, the sound-design team can start working on some elements. For example in *Chat*, the lead character who suffers from photophobia, has scenes where he loses his protective sunglasses and is exposed to natural daylight, causing disorientation and confusion. The sound design team started working on sample effects as soon as the initial spotting was complete, as they did not need a perfectly locked cut in order to brainstorm concepts.

As the edit completes, the locked reels get turned over one by one to the sound design team. At that point they can start dialogue cleanup and mixing, which involves smoothing the dialogue across cuts, making it consistent, and making final decisions about what can be salvaged and what can be ADR'd. They can do this work reel by reel, while they wait for a full cut to be issued. They can also at this stage start inserting premade effects from sound libraries in appropriate places in order to complete what is missing from location sound.

Once the entire film is locked, the foley team comes in, and foleys the entire film, completing all the missing sound effects. At that point the actors also need to get scheduled for ADR. The process of bringing all the pieces together is in motion.

The sound design team then assembles all the elements, including the score tracks that need to be delivered by the end of the foley process. The team then premixes the film, prepping for the final sound-mixing session, which usually lasts anywhere from a couple days to a couple weeks. This is the point where the director sits in, and each piece of the film is adjusted for the final mix. Finally the final mix is rendered and delivered to the editor, who then issues the final render of the film.

Foreign distribution requirements impose getting separate music and effects tracks delivered so the dialogue can be separated for dubbing purposes. Your sound-design team should be delivering four tracks to you — a fully mixed track, dialogue only, sound effects only, and score only. One thing to note is that on large productions, the effects track is usually fully rebuilt (meaning that every single sound other than dialogue is rebuilt using foley or sound libraries, and added to that track). On lower budget films, however, due to financial and time constraints, the sound-design team utilizes whatever sounds can be salvaged from the production track and does not replace those. For example, if your characters are eating in a restaurant and the location sound of the forks and knives clinking against the plates is usable (and mixed with the dialogue) they will use it. What this means is that if/when you remove the dialogue track for dubbing that sound will also be gone. The music and effects (M&E) track that is delivered is considered a partial M&E, and will likely need to be completed for full international delivery. If you have the budget to pay for a full M&E initially, it's the better solution to consider, though it is perfectly acceptable, as I did with *Chat*, to just do a partial M&E and get the full one completed once an international sales deal is presented.

4. Color Correction and Visual Effects (VFX)

The last piece of the puzzle is the combination of color correction and visual effects (VFX).

Color correction is the process in which the picture captured on location is enhanced and adjusted to give the film its final look. It can make a tremendous difference when all is said and done, and any good director of photography will shoot the film in a manner that is conducive to adjusting as much as needed in post.

Once the edit is locked, the cut is usually turned over to a colorist (in my case, it was the director of photography). The DP and director will convey to the colorist what they intended the various scenes to look like, and the colorist then applies sample grades and sends some screen shots for validation. Color correction can be used in many ways and for many purposes. Sometimes the DP already came close to the look he was seeking by using in camera filters and effects, and all the colorist had to do was adjust contrast and light color balance. In other cases, the color correction process can drastically change the look of a scene such as making a bright scene dark, or adding a strong color hue to a scene or the entire film.

Other tools in the colorist's arsenal include putting the focus on one area or another of the screen using masks and vignettes, and sometimes adding basic effects such as a glow to scenes that require it.

For more complex effects, a visual effects artist usually gets involved. You might be wondering why a $50,000 film that consists of mostly dialogue would need visual effects. When people think of VFX they think of robots, spaceships, and explosions. The truth is, VFX can come in handy for much more trivial matters even on a low-budget film. The following are some scenarios where you might need VFX:

- Correcting blemishes: For example, the boom drops into a shot that you really want to keep. Rather than using a lesser take, you can usually have a VFX artist take out that boom, or correct any other technical issues that may make the footage difficult to use.

- Removing unwanted branding: As you may know (and as art directors are well aware of), you cannot display any brands without clearance (which is usually next to impossible to obtain when you're a small independent production). Despite your art crew's best efforts inevitably a logo or two will likely be missed and remain present in the final cut. The VFX artist can touch up these shots and make the brands unrecognizable.

- Supplementing or correcting art shortfalls during the shoot: With *Roundabout American*, we had a shot at a car dealership where the focus was on the billboard display at the entrance. The art department had prepped a sign that turned out to be too small to read in the wide shot we had set up. It would have taken the crew several hours we didn't have to rebuild something larger. After realizing this, I decided to drop the matter knowing that we could rebuild what we wanted in VFX later. The beauty of modern software is that a capable VFX artist can make almost any adjustment to any shot even if it's handheld or had movement in post. If you know on set that the shot will have to be touched it up, it is wise to shoot at least one take either static or at least not handheld, as it will greatly minimize the amount of work required to touch it up.

- Blood effects are another very common use of VFX nowadays. Anyone who has worked with squibs and other practical effects knows the drawbacks of those. Notably that in order to get an impression that will read on camera of blood spattering as the result of a gunshot wound, you need to provision for an amount of blood that will likely repaint any room you're in unless it's very large, and spray the camera and crew with a copious amount of red liquid. The alternative is to use squibs that contain only a small amount of blood that is just enough to show the impact and stain the clothing, and then add the spraying effect later in post.

For all these reasons, VFX will likely come into play at one point or another. If the work you need is simple, you can probably get a student to do most of it at a reasonably low cost, especially if at least one of the shots involves more than just correcting blemishes and making logos disappear (in this scenario he or she is unlikely to end up with anything really usable for a reel).

Color correction and VFX can usually take place at the same time, and can occur simultaneously with all the sound work since they don't involve retiming the cut. The only caveat is that VFX shots will need to be marked, and that the VFX artist will need to turn it in completed to the colorist prior to him or her completing the grading work so he or she can apply the grades to the shots that had effects applied.

5. Putting It All Together and Rendering the Cut

After all the above steps have been completed, the postproduction supervisor (who is often the director or producer on a micro-budget film) should have the following elements at his or her disposal:

- A fully graded cut with VFX shots inserted. This is usually returned in the form of a stripped down Final Cut Pro or Premiere project that only contains the color renders, with one sequence per reel.

- A complete audio mix of the film, delivered either as one track per reel, or sometimes delivered as one long track for the entire film (since the audio transitions often bleed from reel to reel).

The goal is then to assemble all reels into a single sequence, underlay the final audio (and mute any location tracks that may still be present under the reels). You will then want to render a high-resolution master of the film in the original compression format that was used for the editing process. This will be a very large file (at least 100 GB for a film shot in HD) that will be the final master you use to produce all other versions.

From there it is usually recommended to generate an H264 compressed version for web, which can, for example, be placed on Vimeo behind password protection for distribution to sales agents or film festivals. The master should be used for DVD and Blu-ray production as well.

I cannot stress enough the importance of quality control at this stage. Once you have produced a master, several people (the director, producer, and editor) need to sit down and look for any potential glitches or issues both on the sound and visual levels, so these can be corrected prior to DVD or Blu-ray issuing. Even though you might think you have looked over the film 1,000 times, there is always the risk that something got messed up in color correction, during VFX, or in the final mix. You want to spend the two hours to give yourself peace of mind and make sure you're not starting production on a thousand Blu-ray copies that will all include a glitch.

Marketing and Distribution

This chapter was written by our guest author, Carolina Posse, who is an award-winning media producer and educator. She has worked in the arts nonprofit sector as a Programming Manager and Interim Director of the Chicago Latino Film Festival. She has served on juries for the Sundance Institute, Latino Public Broadcasting (LPB), and the Independent Television Service (ITVS). She is currently the film curator for Mostra: Brazilian Film Series. Mostra is a film festival presented in cooperation with Partners of the Americas Illinois-Sao Paulo Chapter. Carolina has guest lectured for educational and governmental institutions and she is full-time faculty member in the Cinema Art + Science department of Columbia College Chicago. Carolina holds a BA in film from Columbia College and a Masters of Arts Management from Columbia College.

Your film is complete. What to do next? Most textbook manuals about film marketing and distribution will insist on the 50 percent rule. The 50 percent rule is the principle that says that you should allocate 50 percent of your budget to getting the movie made, and 50 percent to marketing and distribution (i.e., getting your movie sold). In other words, you should have an amount of money dedicated to promoting and marketing your film equal to the amount you spent to make it.

Although this is the rule that has been traditionally followed by studios for major motion pictures and for intermediate size independent films alike, and probably the ideal route to follow, it is rarely practical or feasible for micro-budget films. When you have $50,000 to make a film, it's an impossibility to set aside half that sum for marketing. The budget will be so tight that you will need to reserve almost all of it to get the film in the can. Doing otherwise would be foolish.

However, you also need to be cognizant of the fact that without any marketing budget the film is unlikely to find an audience.

When I was making my films I modified the 50 percent rule to become the 5 percent or $5,000 rule. The idea being to reserve 5 percent of the budget or $5,000 (whichever is greater) for marketing and distribution. This is the bare minimum percentage you will want (and owe to yourself) to do when the movie is complete so you can submit it to some of the top-tier film festivals, and send it to distributors.

If you don't reserve even 5 percent, you will likely need to find it when the film is complete. This is an acceptable option — perhaps running a Kickstarter campaign for $5,000 finishing funds, or going back to your investors for the additional amount.

If you have a budget greater than $100,000, then it's worth reserving some extra money for promotional efforts in order to maximize the impact you'll make at large film festivals, or to four wall a screening in New York or LA. When you "four-wall" a movie, you are essentially paying to screen your movie in an established movie theater. This is usually done for a fee but sometimes can be done for a cut of the door take. You then advertise and try to get a strong turn out. You also attempt to get critiques to come and review the movie. You are essentially bypassing the traditional process of a distributor making you an offer. It's more proactive. You're going out and doing this, making it happen, without waiting for a distributor. There are new Internet services such as Tugg (/www.tugg.com) that allow you, through social media, to find 200 people in, say, the New York area who agree to pay to see your movie. You then make a deal with a large movie chain to screen your movie on one of its screens. Or you directly approach the movie theater owner and find an off-night to screen it for a reasonable fee.

How does the $5,000 break down? Well, in order to submit to all the major film festivals (more on that in section 1.) you'll need at least $3,000. You'll want to mass produce DVDs and Blu-rays to send to festivals and distributors, which will cost another $500. The last $1,500 will go into miscellaneous expenses such as postage, and making posters and flyers for the film festivals. By mass produce here, we are talking about making enough copies to send to the film festivals. This is completely dependent on your budget. For *Chat*, we had an initial film festival budget of $2,000 dollars. Therefore, we produced enough DVDs to cover the submissions. Not to be forgotten are the promised DVDs you'll need for the Kickstarter campaign. All those people who ponied up $25 want their T-shirts and DVDs! A Blu-ray costs more so you would send them a DVD if possible, unless Blu-ray was specified.

1. Distribution

The invention of the Kinetoscope in the 1890s by Thomas A. Edison and William Dickson ignited the motion-picture entertainment industry. The Kinetoscope was a motion-picture film projector wherein a single filmstrip passed in front of a lens and an electric lightbulb. A single audience member commonly paid a nickel to look through a peephole and see the moving image. Imagined as a scientific tool or perhaps a novelty for the wealthy, Edison imagined an exclusive market for his invention. Entrepreneurs quickly imagined much more.

As the film industry boomed, numerous variations of the Kinetoscope quickly emerged leading Edison to file lawsuit after lawsuit, and engender great enemies. Edison desired to monopolize the film distribution industry and be its only benefactor, but many competitors forged in the tough ethnic city ghettos and buoyed by rapidly expanding fortunes from operating "Nickelodeons" were rising and combative. Between 1910 and 1930 Nickelodeon and theatrical revenue built major studios. Some that still stand strong today are household names such as Universal Pictures, Paramount Pictures, 20th Century Fox, United Artists, Warner Bros., MGM and Columbia Pictures. Eventually, smaller operators such as Walt Disney, Samuel Goldwyn, and David Selznick began to produce and distribute their own productions as well.

The vertical integration of financing, production, distribution, and exhibition of the motion picture was dominated by these companies until 1948 when the US government made the studios divest from their theaters in a case known as "The Paramount Decree." The court decided studios operated a monopoly stranglehold on what and when theaters exhibited, and effectively "walled out" small and independent producers. Divestment was ordered to encourage competition. The ruling also had the ironic effect of cleaving the pioneers of the studio system, such as William Fox, Adolph Zukor, the Warners, Marcus Loew, and Carl Laemmle from their origins as Nickelodeons barons.

As the old "movie moguls" drifted from influence, and television bit into viewing habits once exclusive to theaters, finances shifted. Theater attendance showed the beginnings of decline and studios began to sell off their pre-1948 libraries to television outfits no longer tearfully resisting the upstart fledgling broadcast industry. In this period, an innovative form of film finance began to sneak into the industry, and the practice called "presale" came into existence. Presale is selling the distribution rights of a movie to countries outside the United States before the movie is even produced. Orson Welles is credited as one of the early pioneers and benefactors of this practice.

By the 1960s, classic Hollywood in spirit, practice, and aesthetic appeal was all but extinct precipitating younger "hipper" independent filmmakers' emergence and major studios' collaborations with unknown directors such as Francis Ford Coppola, Martin Scorsese, Sydney Lumet, Woody Allen, and notable others. Other changes included low-budget movies being theatrically distributed and screened throughout the world as well as film festivals becoming more popular and decisive.

The major Hollywood studios kept alive by the films of New Guard invested in higher budget movies in the 1970s and what we know as the "blockbuster" was born. Hits such as *Jaws* from Steven Spielberg, *Star Wars* from George Lucas, and the "disaster-film genre" are memorable examples. Competition became fierce among the studios. Everyone had to have their blockbuster accompanied by technological advances such as Sensurround, 3D, and Quadraphonic. Larger spectacles led to larger production budgets, which led to larger marketing budgets designed to fill seats. Organically the concept of the franchise became prevalent as audiences became fanatically loyal to stories and each edition laid the groundwork for future attendance. Sequels seldom did as well as their predecessors but predictably better than unknown commodities. Movie budgets increased and American movies became more popular abroad. The concept of "home video" became standard and the VHS tape and Betamax were released, the former being the most popular in the US, albeit of lesser quality. Variations of the VHS became available in an attempt to better the quality of the video.

In the 1980s Orion Pictures emerged a leader of the "mini-major" studio movement with a taste for edgy content. New talent followed suit and filmmakers such as Jim Jarmush, Spike Lee, Steven Soderbergh, the Coen Brothers, David Lynch, and John Sayles found international acclaim. Other directors such as Jonathan Demme, Oliver Stone, and James Cameron created work with Orion Pictures.

Subscription cable services such as HBO, Showtime, and The Movie Channel soon followed, gained popularity, and began offering 24-hour schedules. Video rental companies boomed: Blockbuster, Hollywood Video, and hundreds of "Mom and Pop" shops served an insatiable public. Moreover, obscure films that were not released theatrically could be found on VHS.

Audiences wanted better sound and image so laser discs were launched with selected titles but the format never fully captured audience imagination. The movie was divided onto both sides of the disc. Laser-disc players required owners to flip the disc over to continue viewing, much like a music record. Later, more expensive laser-disc players entered the market capable of reading both sides of the disc without disruption, but it was too late. Led by the cultural acceptance, design, and functionality of the compact disc, in 1996 the DVD rapidly became popular boasting high-quality image and sound, and bonus material particularly attractive to cinephiles.

The decline of the in-store rental began in the early 1990s, when cable increased its capability and presence. Pay-per-view was at its peak offering mainly sports shows. Channels such as Sundance and IFC were launched. Home-movie viewing was increasing, and DVD sales were through the roof, while theater attendance continued to decline. Micro-distribution companies became successful and well-known. Companies such as Miramax, Focus Features, Paramount Vantage, led the charge. Technology grew faster and less expensive and audiences preferred buying DVDs and not renting them. Video-rental stores begun closing, and in the early 2000s Netflix launched a new concept of DVD rental: No late fees and a convenient USPS cyclical mail service. This concept drove Blockbuster into bankruptcy.

The 21st Century ushered in "streaming" movies through the Internet as the preferred method for viewing motion pictures. Distributors such as Netflix have been able to expand to many countries. Movies are uploaded to servers and become available to audiences in minutes. Movies are more accessible and the selection of titles is immense. However, independent filmmakers still struggle to find distribution for their works. Outlets such as Netflix carry distribution agreements with the major studios and production companies from Hollywood, making it ironically reminiscent of the restrictive practices that led to the 1948 Paramount Decree for a previous generation of independent filmmakers to distribute their work in mainstream outlets. Boutique distribution companies are filling that gap. Today, Video on Demand is a fast-growing method and distributors are always looking for a faster way to meet the audiences demand and secure larger profits.

1.1 Distribution basics

Major studios and large production companies release their own movies and may acquire the rights of other films. They have divisions that specialize in acquisitions and distribution. These companies also have established deals with foreign distributors mainly through negotiated presale deals controlling the distribution opportunities. Major studios have successful and unsuccessful films. Financial losses are offset against the financial successes. Studios spend lots of money in advertising and have deals with theaters all over the world, therefore obliging them to deliver on a set number of movies annually.

As mentioned earlier, the success of companies such as Miramax energized the independent filmmaker, prompting many major studios to open their own independent divisions. Distribution companies took shape such as THINKFilm, Lionsgate, Pegasus Entertainment, Rogue Pictures, Focus Features, Magnolia Pictures, and more. However, several business models were not sustainable but possessed attractive film catalogs and thus were absorbed by another company.

Unless an independent film has won awards at prestigious festivals, it will most likely not get a theatrical distribution offer. Filmmakers have to find other ways of distributing their films and boutique distribution companies with streaming services are, to date, the most efficient way to do so.

Advances for low-budget films are also rare. Usually distributors acquire the rights of a movie with no money up front with an average 60/40 split in revenue. The average contract is five to seven years, and the filmmaker is responsible for a list of deliverables within a specific period of time.

There is no standard deal. It basically depends on how much risk the distributor is willing to assume and how confident it is in recouping its investment. Predictably, with an independent film without bankable stars, the distributor will take a small risk, if any. Notwithstanding, the independent filmmaker can tip the scale with major critical response from a major festival.

Distributors calculate their offers by evaluating production budgets, marketing costs, and profit projections of similar movies from recent years.

2. Film Festivals

Film Festivals are expensive enterprises that rely on diverse and multiple revenue streams that include submission fees, sponsorship, grants from governments and/or foundations, individual donations, and ticket sales. Their expenses are quite high. Theater rentals, advertising, printing, temporary staffing, salaries, vehicle rentals, and VIP perks, provided in a short dense time frame, are costly.

The film festival industry has grown exponentially in the United States and worldwide. New film festivals are appearing every month because the mass of content that's being produced nowadays is so vast that it needs an ever-growing pool of venues to screen at.

Building an intelligent film festival campaign can be tricky if you have a large festival budget, but it becomes very straightforward if your budget is limited.

2.1 The different levels of film festivals

Submissions to most active film festivals are federated mostly through one website — Withoutabox.com, which is now a subsidiary of IMDB and Amazon. Withoutabox provides a great service free of charge for the filmmaker, allowing you to centralize your project details in one spot, and then submit your film quickly and efficiently to multiple venues. It will also host your film online for festival judges to view, rather than having to send Blu-rays and DVDs manually.

If you log in to Withoutabox and create a project, you will then be offered hundreds upon hundreds of possible venues you can submit your film. How do you choose? Over the years I've come up with the following four tiers for film festivals.

Keep in mind that most film festivals have several deadlines — an early bird, a regular, and a late deadline. It's always recommended to submit by the earliest deadline available, for two reasons. First, the submission price increases with each deadline, and the early bird deadline can sometimes be 30 or 40 percent less expensive than the late deadline. Second, most festivals don't just wait until the end to select films. They fill slots as they go along, whenever they deem a film is worthy of their event. This means that the later you submit, the more of these slots will have been filled. Concurrently most people tend to be late in the game and submit later rather than earlier. As a result, the closer you are to the final cut off, more films will be competing and fewer slots will be available.

2.1a Tier 1 festivals

Tier 1 is five festivals. Sundance, Berlin, Cannes, Venice, and Toronto. These are the festivals where acceptance may bring you both glory and a sale, and the most reputed festivals in the world. They're also the ones where your chances of getting in are exponentially smaller than any other.

Back in 1991, the Sundance Film Festival had 250 film submissions, of which 134 were screened. Your chances of getting in were pretty good at that time; the odds against you were only two to one. By 1996, the number of submissions increased to 1,950, and the number of films screened to 184. The odds against you were ten to one. Fast forward to 2014, the festival received 12,218 submissions, and screened 186. Your chances of acceptance now are 1 in 66. Think about that — for each film that gets accepted, 65 others get rejected! Similar statistics apply to the other festivals in this list, which is why even though you should absolutely submit to all five, you shouldn't count on acceptance, no matter how good you think your film is.

This may not make me friends in the festival circuit, but after years of submitting both my shorts and my features to hundreds of festivals, my conclusion is: It's really only worth submitting to the Tier 1 and Tier 2 film festivals, unless you are looking for a local screening or for festival laurels to add at the beginning of the movie.

Submitting only to Tier 1 and Tier 2 festivals will likely eat up most or all of the $3,000 you can spend if your entire marketing and distribution budget is $5,000. Tier 1 or 2 festivals will land you a solid chance of finding distribution or getting noticed, and you should submit to every single one of them.

2.1b Tier 2 festivals

Tier 2 comprises about 20 to 30 festivals. They are major, internationally recognized venues. These don't have the ultimately glamorous appeal of the first five in Tier 1, but these can land you a distribution deal or, at the very least, a notable entry on your film's résumé. The list evolves over the years as some festivals gain more recognition than others, but some of them include Tribeca, Slamdance, South by Southwest, or AFI FEST are staples you don't want to miss.

2.1c Tier 3 festivals

Tier 3 expands to smaller regional festivals, of which there are hundreds. This list really depends on the film, as these festivals tend to sometimes be geared towards specific genres. Ideally when researching these on Withoutabox, I include only festivals that have at least a five-year history, and seem to have a legitimate structure behind them (i.e., supported by a city, or an organization).

The Tier 3 festivals have a lot of merit, and in no way am I trying to denigrate them, but realistically most of these don't have the ability to generate a substantial audience for the films they showcase, and will not necessarily advance you or your film.

I have attended a lot of these venues and met the organizers, and they are generally people who put a lot of heart in their work and show much more respect for the filmmakers than the Tier 1 or Tier 2 festivals ever will. However, if you're on a tight budget, you need to consider what will provide you with the best chance at getting your film noticed and Tier 3 may not be it. However, these festivals can provide you with the opportunity to screen your film in your city, so I would encourage you to submit to Tier 3 film festivals in your hometown, or any city where you feel you can bring in a crowd. If you are able to fill the room, these festivals will give you an opportunity to showcase your work, and possibly get an award.

Another reason to stay away from Tier 3 festivals is that most Tier 1 and Tier 2 festivals require the film to be a local premiere at least in their city in order to consider it. In other words, if you submit to Tier 3 festivals in LA and get accepted, you've now essentially killed your chances for consideration at AFI FEST or any other Los Angeles-based festival.

2.1d Tier 4 festivals

Tier 4 is the rest of the flock, which includes hundreds and hundreds of minor film festivals, some of which are simply scams that collect submission fees from filmmakers and screen a few films in a remote venue without anyone in the room. Beware in particular of festivals that imitate the name of a famous festival by changing a minor word — a notorious scam. Always make sure you are submitting to the fest you intend to submit.

The Tier 4 film festivals should generally be avoided as they will usually bring no benefit at all and will just eat up the cost you've allocated to submissions.

2.2 How festivals select films

The majority of festivals have an open-submission process where film-makers pay a fee, complete a submission form, and submit the film for consideration. Others work under an "invitation only" policy.

Some festivals have a selection committee that meets and debate the selection, while others rely on the programmer and festival director to make the final selections.

It is very common for festival representatives that include the festival director, programmer, or members of the selection committee to travel to other festivals from around the world to select films and invite them to exhibit at their own festival. Therefore, it is very common to see some of the same faces and films at large prestigious festivals. Programmers and festival directors tend to know each other, and engage in cordial competition. Festival programmers want to discover the new voice and new filmmaker so world premieres are very valuable in the festival circuit (with national or regional premieres valued as well). Festivals like premieres because premieres represent a sophisticated selection process, a prestigious asset to festival attendees, and the possibility of worldwide or significant press attention.

"To Premiere" means to publicly and professionally screen for the first time. Designations such as "World," "National," and "City" premieres are dependent on the order, timing, and prestige of the venue exhibiting the film. Either way, to premiere gives value to the movie and the festival.

Festivals can be either competitive or noncompetitive. Competitive festivals are very selective of their films. They strongly prefer premieres and it is very common for them to impose strict guidelines in their categories that all the filmmakers are obliged to follow. Examples likely include a first-time feature film director and the film has to be a World Premiere. Noncompetitive festivals are likely of smaller scope and at times affiliated with colleges or universities.

The bottom line is that filmmakers need to research film festivals and strategize before sending their film for consideration. Questions to consider include:

- What is the festival's mission statement?
- What kind of films has it included in the past?
- Is it competitive or not?

- What are the deadlines?

- What are the fees?

- What are the deliverables? (See section 3. for more details.)

- Is the festival well-respected and well-known?

- What kinds of awards are given?

- Does the festival invite the filmmaker to accompany his or her work?

The average life span of a film in the festival circuit is two years. Once the film has a World Premiere in a festival the two-year life span begins; therefore, it is very important for filmmakers to design a film festival screening strategy taking into consideration the questions mentioned above.

3. Deliverables for Film Festivals and Distributors

Deliverables is a term commonly used both in the film festival circuit and with distributors. Once the film has been accepted to a film festival, the programming department will contact the filmmaker and confirm its participation. Prior to the festival announcing its film selection, it confirms with the filmmaker that the print or screening copy, and titling and press materials can be delivered on time. The film can be delivered to the festival by uploading it to a server, sending a Blue-ray or DVD, and, on occasion, a film print (generally 35 mm or 16 mm).

If the film is in English, and the festival is in the United States, there is no need to subtitle the film; however, if screening in other countries, filmmakers may need to subtitle. The most common subtitles are English, French, Spanish, Portuguese, and Mandarin. The festival will generally detail its subtitle requirements.

In addition, the festival will need the aspect ratio and sound specs as well as the Electronic Press Kit (EPK). The EPK is a digital version of the film's basic information (see section 3.1).

3.1 Key elements in an electronic press kit (EPK)

The electronic press kit (EPK) is an important opportunity for the filmmakers to show their creativity and taste. It is an extension of the film itself and it needs to be consistent with the website and other promotional and marketing materials. There are EPKs that can be of very high-elaborate quality with multiple pages, but simplicity can go a long way too, especially if resources are tight.

The "one-sheet" is the visual summary of the film. Think of it as a single-page thematic synopsis in picture and text. Even if the film is a short subject, every production benefits from possessing a one-sheet. Be sure to include a title and the "billing block," which is the list of the principle creatives and talent behind the film. Commonly that is the production company, director, cast, writer, producer, executive producers, director of photography, production designer, editor, composer, costume designer and casting director. Some of these may vary depending on the film. It is also customary to show who owns the copyright and in what year the film was released.

On the back of the one-sheet or on another page, the logline and brief synopsis are included (see Chapter 3 for more details). Some stills from the film and some behind-the-scene shots are also common. In addition, the film specs are listed. Film Specs are the technical specifications of the project — format, aspect ratio, sound, length, subtitles, color and/or black and white, country of origin, and year of release.

Headshots and succinct bios of the main cast are very common in addition to the same for the director, writer, and producer. At times, other department heads are included in this section of the EPK but it depends on the project and their marketable status.

A key element in the EPK is the contact information of the production company or producer, so another festival programmer or distributor will know whom to contact.

It is important to point out that each festival handles its submission process differently and filmmakers need to read the guidelines carefully before submitting. As mentioned earlier, a popular website used by filmmakers is Withoutabox.com an online service that allows you to search for festivals, prepare a general film submission application, upload a screener of the film, and an EPK.

A screener refers to a copy of the film. Some festivals may require a screener in a tangible form, such as a DVD, while others may ask you to upload the film on sites like Vimeo or YouTube but with password protection. If the film is made available online for public viewing, festivals may lose interest in screening it because the film is deemed to have lost its value and prestige.

Withoutabox.com has a vast selection of festivals but it is not the only source. Reading online publications such as *Filmmaker Magazine* or Indiewire can help filmmakers find festivals and learn some of the trends in the industry. These are just a couple of examples; there is plenty of material online that can be quite helpful.

3.2 Deliverables for distributors

The list of deliverables for a distributor is much longer than for the film festival. The film festival is screening the film once or twice at its event, in comparison to the distributor who is licensing the rights of the movie for an extended period of time.

All deliverables vary but here are some of the most common examples used: The list should be detailed and included at the end of the distribution agreement. It is key for the producer who enters into the contract with the distributor to know precisely what he or she is responsible for and committing to in the agreement.

Distributors will require all contracts pertaining to intellectual property ownership and rights to privacy. Common contracts include all chain of title agreements, such as the following:

- Copyright ownership.

- Option purchase agreement.

- Depiction releases, if applicable.

- All writers' work-for-hire agreements (this can be one or multiple agreements, as it is not unusual for more than one writer to contribute to a screenplay).

- All Certificate of Authorship contracts.

- Writers Guild of America registration.

- All actors contracts.

- Product placement contracts.

- Location releases.

- Music and composers agreements.

- Department head contracts.

- Errors and omissions insurance. The errors and omissions insurance is a type of insurance that protects the production company of any unforeseen claims against the film that have to do with copyright infringement, defamation of character, or invasion of privacy. It is very common for distributors to request proof of this insurance upon signing of the agreement in order to indemnify themselves from any liability claims of this sort.

Besides all copies of the contracts, the distributors will also request a dialogue list (for the purposes of subtitling or dubbing), video, music, and sound FX files, all art work such as the poster, DVD cover, stills, and behind-the-scene files. Also include any press clippings and award information, if available.

4. Film Markets

Contrary to film festivals, film markets are exclusive and are not open to non-industry professionals. To attend a film market, professionals must register beforehand and pay the registration fee to receive the pass and access the event. Fees vary in cost but tend to be pricey for the purpose of maintaining the market purely for professionals in the film industry.

A simple way to understand a film market is that its purpose is to facilitate deal making between buyers and sellers. The buyers are distributors, while the sellers are producers, production companies, and/ or micro-distributors.

The biggest film market in the United States is the American Film Market (AFM). It is an event that takes place in November every year at The Loews Santa Monica Beach Hotel. The AFM is produced by the Independent Film & Television Alliance, and was launched in 1981.

Some festivals offer a market component to them similar to Cannes, Toronto, Berlin, and Montreal. Other markets that are internationally recognized are FILMART (Hong Kong), CineMart (Rotterdam), and IN-PUT (different locations around the world) to name a few.

In a film market, attendees may find a distributor for their film or financing for their project. Markets have an international appeal, as it's the opportunity for international buyers to do deals with American producers and production companies, and find coproduction deals for financing. In film markets, the presale is a very common yet highly valued deal.

Presales, as explained earlier, are a way to finance a film by selling the rights to distribute the movie in a territory outside the United States such as Latin America, Asia, and Europe. Established distribution companies that know their market well handle these territories, and the companies have robust credit lines to borrow money from private lenders or banks. Presales usually occur for production budgets of more than $2 million with projects containing well-known talent attached. Presale deals are a risk to the foreign distributors so they rely on marquee talent that is well-known in their territories to hedge their investment; action films with A- List actors usually do very well in theaters abroad. The distribution company gets revenue through ticket sales and repays the money to the bank within a short period of time.

Film markets are busy business gatherings at which many screenings take place. Informal and formal meetings happen throughout and wherever an opportunity may present itself. The term "elevator pitch" comes from such a dynamic. The idea is to close the deal before the next floor arrives. Therefore, it is key to also attend the market with a strategy. Who is attending, what companies may be interested in the project, and when they would be there. It's critical to bring screeners and EPKs ready to hand out.

5. Representation

Artist and labor representation is very common in the film industry, and it ties to distribution either by engaging professionals to represent you, by negotiating deferred payments, percentage of profits that get split, and so forth. The most common forms of entities that a producer encounters and negotiates are discussed in the following sections.

5.1 Unions and guilds

Unions and guilds protect the workplace and economic interests of labor and performers. Although budget size has a proportional effect on the presence or not of union-grade labor on a set, producers of low-budget films would have a greater likelihood of working with the Screen Actors Guild (SAG-AFTRA). SAG represents all actors, and it's the only union that offers different contracts to producers depending on the scope and budget of their project. Even film students can hire union actors to work on their films, but the producer of the project needs to notify the union and sign the proper paperwork. This paperwork establishes the producer as "signatory to the union." In summary, the producer agrees to follow union rules and regulations.

5.2 Sales agents

Sales agents are found in all film markets. They represent producers and projects in search of financing or distribution, or both. They can work independently or with a company, and they work for commission.

5.3 Entertainment attorneys

All talent will need counsel in their career. A practiced, impartial, and well-versed entertainment lawyer can provide advice on the process or industry best practices. Attorneys can help to get a better deal or represent a client in a legal dispute.

An attorney typically requires an engagement letter to be signed by you. This letter will detail the terms of engagement and the fees. Attorney's fees can be costly, but attorneys have the liberty to represent in a pro-bono basis. They may want to do it for the experience, or train a junior attorney in the firm, or simply out of kindness. Pro-bono is common but it depends on the case.

Retainer fees are not uncommon but usually indicate the attorney envisions a long drawn-out process with doubtful or miniscule financial gain.

5.4 Talent agents and managers

Talent agents represent actors, directors, and cinematographers. They may work independently or with a company, and they work purely on commission. Managers have more flexibility and fees can be salaried, flat, or by commission.

5.5 Publicists

Publicists manage the image of their clients in public. Publicists can represent a film festival, a company, or an individual.

6. Types of Distribution Agreements

It is important to clarify that all contracts and all deals are customized to the project and the parties involved. There is no such thing as the "cookie-cutter" deal as everything is negotiable. However, there are some common distribution terms used in the industry. Use these as your starting place.

Note that it is rare for low-budget films to have any agreements like the ones mentioned in the following sections. Producers will more likely use other methods of financing such as soft-monies, private equity, and crowd sourcing (as mentioned in Chapter 5). In low-budget films, producers heavily rely on taking the film festival route so the film can receive some recognition, and hopefully win a few awards and be discovered by a distributor. Producers can also attend markets and send the film for consideration to distributors. The bottom line, it is the producer's role to find one distributor or several distributors to have the film available in the marketplace.

It is important to point out that if the low-budget film was financed with any type of private equity, there are investors out there waiting to have their investment back with interest otherwise known as return on investment (ROI).

6.1 Production Finance Distribution (PFD) Agreement

A Production Finance Distribution (PFD) Agreement, is used when a studio hires a production company to produce a film. The studio finances and distributes the film, maintains sole ownership of the film, and has all control.

6.2 Negative Pick-up Agreement

In a Negative Pick-up Agreement the film is financed through a studio but the production company does not receive the money in advance. The production company borrows the funds and secures a Completion Bond Insurance policy as a hedge against failure to complete or gross schedule or budget overages. A Completion Bond is a type of insurance that assures the completion and delivery of the film. The lender will require this type of insurance, as having the finished film is the only way to recoup the loan. As there are a few more parties involved in the Negative Pick-up Agreement, the deal is a bit more complicated than the Production Finance Distribution (PFD) agreement.

6.3 Presale Agreement

A Presale Agreement, as was mentioned in section 4., is a deal in which a foreign distributor pays for the licensed rights to screen the film prior to production. Foreign distributors from many different countries make a pledge that is known as the Minimum Guarantee (MG). The MG is a flat amount negotiated per market. As different countries commit to an MG, the producer is tasked with raising the production funds, or a large percentage of it, through multiple countries.

6.4 Terms to understand in the contracts

All distribution contracts are customizable, but these are some key clauses in each contract that need to be addressed.

All distribution contracts will ask the producer to waive his or her "Droit Morale" (Moral Right), a French term that protects the artists' vision manifested in the creative choices of the film.

In terms of accounting, distributors should commit to send the producer accounting reports on a quarterly or an annual basis during the duration of the contract. These reports should reflect the revenue streams and any deductions to the gross receipts. The producer shall maintain the right to audit the accounting reports.

6.4a Rights

As a film is a form of intellectual property protected under the *Copyright Act*, the copyright owner has a bundle of rights. These include the right to copy, to prepare derivative works, to distribute copies of the work, to publicly display the work, and to rent, lease, or lend the work. In a distribution agreement these rights are clearly stated; otherwise, the distributor cannot monetize and exploit the film. The producer can agree to transfer the copyright and "bundle" the rights to the distributor, or he or she can slice the rights. The rights can be sliced in two different ways:

- **Exclusive or nonexclusive**: If a producer agrees to an exclusive deal with the distributor, the distributor is the only company in the world that carries the film. A nonexclusive deal means that there are several distributors capable of carrying the film.

- **Domestic or foreign territories**: In distribution the term "domestic" always refers to the United States and Canada, while foreign refers to all the other countries.

6.4b Platforms

The largest platform for releasing a movie is still theatrical, as it's the most prestigious, difficult to achieve, and the studios pretty much control the theater chains. Some theater art houses might be more interested in screening a low-budget film, but again after the film has been recognized in the festival circuit. Awards and prestige get people to purchase tickets. Here is the catch: A low-budget film may screen one day or one week in an art house but not all art houses are distributors, they might be only a theater, so it falls on the producer to serve as the distributor to secure these bookings.

Other options for theatrical releases still exist. Producers of low-budget films may choose to take a high risk and make a deal directly with a theater. As mentioned earlier, this is called "four-walling," which means the producer rents the theater for a period of time and keeps the revenue. The theater makes money up front and keeps the concession. Other times, producers may successfully make a deal with an independent theater chain and split revenue.

The following are some of the other release platforms:

- **Nontheatrical:** This refers to the exploitation of the film in small venues such as universities, colleges, libraries, churches, airlines, and military bases. It does not mean everything else but theatrical.

- **Home video:** This became very popular in the 1970s and it still stands strong today. It is the exploitation of a film through a tangible medium such as cassette, DVD, disk, or flash drive.

- **Video-on-Demand (VOD):** This is a bit more complex and it has truly revolutionized distribution. Unless otherwise explicitly stated in the contract, VOD includes streaming and download; an act that begins when the consumer chooses free of broadcaster scheduling. VOD can be offered through the Internet, television, cable, or satellite. Pay-per-view is a service included in the cable and satellite rights, while television includes all broadcast rights. Today, the tablet, cell phone, and wearables are new screen devices and are being negotiated separately as unique venues.

6.4c Length of time

Distribution agreements used to last at least ten years, but it has become more common to average a five- to seven-year deal. It is also common for the distributor to request a Right of First Refusal clause, in which it gives the distributor the opportunity to make an offer to the producer as an option to renew the contract before the producer accepts another deal somewhere else.

6.4d Distribution fee

The distribution fee is the amount the distributor will make from the gross receipts. The fee is usually a percentage split for the exploitation of the rights. The distributor's fee averages 15 to 30 percent but it all depends on the scope of the project.

Another fee that can be included is the sales agent percentage, which averages 10 to 15 percent,

6.4e Recoupable expenses

The recoupable expenses is an amount the distribution company is pledging it will incur on behalf of marketing the film. Some examples include attending film markets, advertising, and redesign of artwork.

Recoupable expenses do not include overhead costs such as salaries, office rental, or the electric bill of the distributor.

6.4f Right to make changes

The distributor will always want to reserve the right to make changes to the edit. Changes can be made to insert commercials, omit or recut scenes due to content, or to fit the film in a broadcasting slot. The distributor will also want to reserve the right to recreate the artwork, dub the dialogue, and display subtitles.

7. Boutique Distributors

For low-budget films, features, and shorts, online distribution is full of possibilities. Many boutique companies focus on video-on-demand strategies and have a strong catalog to compete with larger outlets such as Netflix.

Researching different companies is how to start. Many boutique distributors are founded by executives who left larger companies, while others were created by a group of filmmakers who got tired of waiting in line. In your research, consider the following before contacting a boutique distributor:

- Who founded the company?

- What is its mission?

- Does it operate with exclusive or nonexclusive rights?

- Does it have a standard revenue split?

- How popular is its website?

- What are the types of films it carries in its catalog?

Thinking outside of domestic territories is helpful. Many countries are investing in digital infrastructure and the Internet is becoming faster. Countries such as Australia, Brazil, and India are vastly growing and Internet access is more common and distributors are expanding. Audiences in Germany, France, Japan, and the United Kingdom have great capability and media content is being uploaded more and more every day. It is a great time for online distribution; this is just the beginning of the many possibilities.

Download kit

Please enter the URL you see in the box below into your computer web browser to access and download the kit.

www.self-counsel.com/updates/diyfilmmaker/15kit.htm

The download kit offers resources that provide insight into the making of a film and an example of a successful script.

β 95